NARCOTICS

Other books in the Drug Education Library series:

Alcohol
Cocaine and Crack
Hallucinogens
Heroin
Marijuana
Nicotine

NARCOTICS

by Pam Walker and Elaine Wood

San Diego • Detroit • New York • San Francisco • Cleveland
New Haven, Conn. • Waterville, Maine • London • Munich

PJC PENSACOLA CAMPUS LRC

© 2003 by Lucent Books. Lucent Books is an imprint of The Gale Group, Inc.,
a division of Thomson Learning, Inc.

Lucent Books® and Thomson Learning™ are trademarks used herein under license.

For more information, contact
Lucent Books
27500 Drake Rd.
Farmington Hills, MI 48331-3535
Or you can visit our Internet site at http://www.gale.com

ALL RIGHTS RESERVED.
No part of this work covered by the copyright hereon may be reproduced or used in any form or by
any means—graphic, electronic, or mechanical, including photocopying, recording, taping, Web distribution or information storage retrieval systems—without the written permission of the publisher.

LIBRARY OF CONGRESS CATALOGING-IN-PUBLICATION DATA

Walker, Pam, 1958–
    Narcotics / by Pam Walker and Elaine Wood.
        v. cm. — (Drug education library)
Includes bibliographical references and index.
Contents: Narcotics, the "milk of paradise"—Search for the perfect pain-killer—Narcotic
addiction and abuse—Treatment and prevention of narcotic addiction—Battle in the drug
war.
    ISBN 1-59018-043-7
    1. Narcotics—Juvenile literature. 2. Narcotic habit—Juvenile literature. [1. Narcotics. 2.
Narcotic habit. 3. Drug abuse.] I. Wood, Elaine, 1950–II. Title. III. Series.
    RM328.W35 2004
    615'.7822—dc21

                                    2003000408

Printed in the United States of America

Contents

Foreword

The development of drugs and drug use in America is a cultural paradox. On the one hand, strong, potentially dangerous drugs provide people with relief from numerous physical and psychological ailments. Sedatives like Valium counter the effects of anxiety; steroids treat severe burns, anemia, and some forms of cancer; morphine provides quick pain relief. On the other hand, many drugs (sedatives, steroids, and morphine among them) are consistently misused or abused. Millions of Americans struggle each year with drug addictions that overpower their ability to think and act rationally. Researchers often link drug abuse to criminal activity, traffic accidents, domestic violence, and suicide.

These harmful effects seem obvious today. Newspaper articles, medical papers, and scientific studies have highlighted the myriad problems drugs and drug use can cause. Yet, there was a time when many of the drugs now known to be harmful were actually believed to be beneficial. Cocaine, for example, was once hailed as a great cure, used to treat everything from nausea and weakness to colds and asthma. Developed in Europe during the 1880s, cocaine spread quickly to the United States where manufacturers made it the primary ingredient in such everyday substances as cough medicines, lozenges, and tonics. Likewise, heroin, an opium derivative, became a popular painkiller during the late nineteenth century. Doctors and patients flocked to American drugstores to buy heroin, described as the optimal cure for even the worst coughs and chest pains.

As more people began using these drugs, though, doctors, legislators, and the public at large began to realize that they were more damaging than beneficial. After years of using heroin as a painkiller, for example, patients began asking their doctors for larger and stronger doses. Cocaine users reported dangerous side effects, including hallucinations and wild mood shifts. As a result, the U.S. government initiated more stringent regulation of many powerful and addictive drugs, and in some cases outlawed them entirely.

A drug's legal status is not always indicative of how dangerous it is, however. Some drugs known to have harmful effects can be purchased legally in the United States and elsewhere. Nicotine, a key ingredient in cigarettes, is known to be highly addictive. In an effort to meet their bodies' demands for nicotine, smokers expose themselves to lung cancer, emphysema, and other life-threatening conditions. Despite these risks, nicotine is legal almost everywhere.

Other drugs that cannot be purchased or sold legally are the subject of much debate regarding their effects on physical and mental health. Marijuana, sometimes described as a gateway drug that leads users to other drugs, cannot legally be used, grown, or sold in this country. However, some research suggests that marijuana is neither addictive nor a gateway drug and that it might actually benefit cancer and AIDS patients by reducing pain and encouraging failing appetites. Despite these findings and occasional legislative attempts to change the drug's status, marijuana remains illegal.

The Drug Education Library examines the paradox of drugs and drug use in America by focusing on some of the most commonly used and abused drugs or categories of drugs available today. By discussing objectively the many types of drugs, their intended purposes, their effects (both planned and unplanned), and the controversies surrounding them, the books in this series provide readers with an understanding of the complex role drugs and drug use play in American society. Informative sidebars, annotated bibliographies, and organizations to contact lists highlight the text and provide young readers with many opportunities for further discussion and research.

Introduction

The Many Faces of Narcotics

Since the earliest times, people have used opium, the parent drug of a group of chemicals called narcotics. Like almost anything, narcotics can be used for good or bad purposes. When used properly, narcotics are valued medications in the treatment of pain. They are the standard against which the effectiveness of other pain treatments are measured. People who suffer from long-term or extreme pain depend on medically prescribed narcotics.

The Grip of Addiction

But these benefits have a cost. In some people, narcotics cause a type of dependence called addiction. Addiction can consume a person, changing personality so drastically that some narcotic addicts have suffered loss of families, friends, jobs, and homes.

One might wonder how anything could take over a person's mind with such power. Some researchers believe that it may be impossible for the nonaddicted to comprehend addiction. According to author Mike Gray's *Drug Crazy,*

> The easiest way to understand the mind of a drug addict is to use food as a metaphor. Imagine you've just been told by the government that food is so bad for you it's been taken off the market. You might be able to handle

it for a couple of days, and after that you wouldn't be able to think about anything else—food—how to get it, where to get it, and where to steal the money now that a hot dog with mustard is suddenly fifty dollars. But even this metaphor is an inadequate measure of the addict's urgency because a junkie, though starving, will trade food for dope.[1]

The dangers of narcotic addiction are many, and they include death. Taking a fatal overdose is easy to do. Overdosing can happen accidentally if a drug addict uses narcotics of unexpected high quality. Victims of narcotic-related deaths include well-known music and movie stars. One of the first was rock singer of the 1960s Janice Joplin, who died of an overdose. Her death was soon followed by the loss of Jim Morrison, lead singer of the

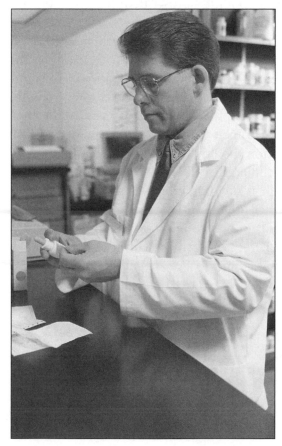

A pharmacist fills a patient's narcotics prescription. If used illegally, narcotics can lead to addiction and even death.

Doors. Since then the list has grown and includes John Belushi, comedian and actor, and guitarist Jonathon Melvoin of Smashing Pumpkins, who both died from an overdose; and musician Jerry Garcia of the Grateful Dead who died from complications of narcotic use.

A Power Painkiller

Despite these grim facts, narcotics are respected drugs that have a role in medicine. A lot of people suffer from the pain of headaches, backaches, muscle pains, neck pains, and long-term health problems like cancer. Doctors treat the most serious of these painful conditions with narcotics because they are extremely effective in reducing pain. Skillfully prescribed, narcotics do not make patients sleepy or confused. Unlike addicts, the patients do not experience the high or euphoria associated with abuse.

Thousands of people benefit from treatment with narcotics for pain relief. Lisa Steinberg, a forty-one-year-old doctor in Maryland and a cancer patient, was unable to walk because of painful growths on the bones in her hips. Steinberg now lives with a small pump implanted in her abdomen that delivers a slow, steady dose of narcotic pain medication directly into her spinal column. The medication has given Steinberg her life back, enabling her to walk and function again, much as she did before she got sick.

Narcotic drugs, whether used legally or illegally, are part of life for hundreds of thousands of people. However, many do not understand the dangers of narcotics. Anyone who uses narcotics can face addiction, overdoses, and other negative consequences whether the drugs are prescribed or used recreationally.

Chapter 1

Narcotics, the "Milk of Paradise"

Since the beginning of time, humans have searched for ways to ease pain, the sensation of suffering or distress. Even though pain is unpleasant, it is an essential feeling; its purpose is to let the body know that something is wrong. Despite this merit, pain can be difficult to endure for long periods of time. Most of the work of early medical practitioners was simply directed at ending pain, and any effective drug was prized. Today, pain is still feared and avoided, and hundreds of medicines and treatments have been developed to treat and prevent it.

There are many classes of drugs used by the medical community to treat pain. Some of the most effective painkillers have limited usefulness because they knock the patient unconscious. Analgesics, drugs that can ease pain without causing unconsciousness, are valued because they allow the patient to continue with day-to-day activities. Scores of different analgesics block pain in a variety of ways. In pharmacology, the study of drugs and medications, analgesics are generally divided into two broad categories: narcotics and the nonnarcotics. Narcotics are the most potent pain relievers known to man. In low doses, they are highly effective analgesics.

Narcotics are a group of drugs with chemical structures similar to that of opium, a medicine derived from the sap of the opium poppy. Some are isolated directly from the opium poppy, but others can be made in the lab. Narcotics derived from the natural plant source are called opiates, and they include opium and its active ingredients, morphine and codeine. Any drug that is made in a lab is described as synthetic, or man-made. Synthetic narcotics are collectively known as opioids and they include heroin, hydrocodone, and fentanyl.

Narcotics are not only prized because they relieve pain; they also change mood and behavior, producing a relaxed feeling of well-being or relief. Therefore, they reduce the anxiety associated with pain. Most patients taking narcotics state that they are experiencing just as much pain as they did without the medication, but they find the pain less troubling.

Drugs classified as narcotics have several other effects on the body. Narcotics constrict the pupils of the eye, slow breathing rate, and widen veins of the skin, making the body look flushed and feel warm. They slow down the digestive system, including the activity of the intestines, and have been used for centuries to treat diarrhea. They have a calming action on coughs and can be administered in their treatment. Narcotics can also cause nausea and vomiting. At high doses, they affect consciousness, making it difficult for a patient to maintain a train of thought without some form of external stimulation. Extremely large amounts can bring on coma or a state of unconsciousness.

Graham Greene, novelist, explains his state of mind after trying opium for the first time:

> My mind felt alert and calm—unhappiness and fear of the future became like something dimly remembered which I had thought important once. I, who feel shy at exhibiting the grossness of my French, found myself reciting a poem of Baudelaire to my companion. When I got home that night, I experienced for the first time the white night of opium. One lies relaxed and wakeful, not desiring sleep. We dread wakefulness when our thoughts are disturbed, but in this state one is calm—it would be wrong even to say one is happy—happiness disturbs the pulse. And then suddenly without warning one sleeps. Never has one slept so deeply a whole night-long

The first narcotics were made from the opium poppy plant. The seedpod of the flower is mixed with other elements to create opium.

sleep, and then the waking and the luminous dial of the clock showing that twenty minutes of so-called real time have gone by.[2]

The First Narcotics

These mind-altering effects were discovered when the first narcotics were derived from the opium poppy, *Papaver somniferum*. Opium poppy plants grow naturally in temperate climates around the world. They bear flowers that range in color from pure white to brilliant purple. The egg-bearing pistil, the female structure, lies at the center of an opium flower. After pollination, eggs begin maturing into seeds within the pistil, which swells to form an oval seedpod. Within a few days, the flower petals fall off leaving the seedpod exposed. The seedpod can be left on the plant, allowing the seeds to finish maturing and dry out. Or, the pod can be scored with shallow cuts of a knife to release opium. Scoring causes a thick, white resin to ooze from the slits. As it contacts the air, the resin darkens and congeals. It is scraped from the seedpod and combined with the resin from other plants to form a ball of crude opium. This is usually processed into forms for eating or smoking.

Opium has been intimately involved in the history of many ancient cultures. The Sumerians, a group who occupied the area of modern day Iraq in 3400 B.C., described the opium poppy as *Hul Gil*, the joy plant. They introduced opium to the Assyrians, who in turn shared it with the Babylonians. The Babylonians passed on their knowledge to the Egyptians.

Opium is featured prominently in Egyptian history. Egyptian records from 1300 B.C. show that opium consumption and trade flourished during the reigns of several famous pharaohs, including Thutmose IV, Akhenaton, and Tutankhamen, or King Tut. Historians have found opium-extracting equipment buried with important rulers, a practice designed to enable the kings to harvest opium in the next life.

Most Egyptian families kept a stock of opium in their homes. A prescription called "Remedy to Prevent the Excessive Crying of Children" was found in one home; the preparation's directions stated that opium should be mixed with "the excretions of flies

The Sumerians (pictured on this panel) made wide use of the opium poppy and introduced it to other ancient cultures.

found on the walls, strained to a pulp, passed through a sieve, and administered on four successive days. The crying will stop at once."[3]

Myths and Medicine

Egyptians carried opium across the Mediterranean Sea to Greece and Rome where the plant became so important that it was incorporated into the mythology of both cultures. In Greece, writings from 600 B.C. refer to the medical use of opium poppies in the treatment of a variety of diseases, and stories of the time abound with references to the drug. According to legend, the mythological healer Aesculapius saved the life of the hero Hippolytus with a medicine that contained only one amazing ingredient. Since statues of Aesculapius show him wearing garlands of opium poppy seedpods, historians believe that the one powerful ingredient was opium. Temples built to honor Aesculapius were tended by physician priests called Aesculapians who were considered to be the best doctors in Greece. When a sick person sought help, an Aesculapian fed the patient a large dose of opium to cause sleep. Upon awakening, the patient reported any dreams experienced under the drug's influence. The physician then prescribed a treatment based on the patient's own opium-induced dreams.

The most famous Aesculapian was Hippocrates (ca. 460–337 B.C.) who is known as the father of medicine. Although Hippocrates frowned on the public's perception of opium as a recreational drug, he did recommend it as a medicine. In his writings, he spoke of opium's curative powers in the treatment of a range of ills, including sleeplessness, various epidemics, and women's problems. One of the last great Aesculapian physicians was Galen (A.D. 131–200), a man who was considered by many to be the greatest medical mind of his time. He made a list of opium's medical uses, explaining how it

> resists poison and venomous bites, cures chronic headache, vertigo, deafness, epilepsy, apoplexy, dimness of sight, loss of voice, asthma, coughs of all kinds, spitting of blood, tightness of breath, colic, the lilac poison, jaundice, hardness of the spleen stone, urinary complaints, fever, dropsies [swelling], leprosies, the trouble with which women are subject, melancholy and all pestilences.[4]

Hippocrates prescribed opium as medicine, but he disapproved of recreational use of the drug.

The Popularity of Opium Smoking

By the seventh century, natives of Turkey had developed a new way to use opium. Instead of eating plant parts or brewing them to make a tea, they found that heating the drug and inhaling the smoke allowed them to experience the benefits of opium much faster. As a consequence, opium's popularity as a recreational drug grew. However, the Turks did not realize that the switch from eating opium to smoking it was more likely to make users dependent on the drug. Within just a few years, opium smoking was wreaking havoc on peoples' lives. Physicians and politicians spoke out against the drug, and opium lost its status as an important medicine in many cultures.

Centuries later, opium once again found favor, this time in Europe. In the late 1500s, Paracelsus, an eccentric physician, philosopher, and healer from Switzerland, developed a new method of consuming opium. He knew that opium's components did not dissolve easily in water because they have a base, or alkaline, nature. He deduced that opium that is consumed is not completely absorbed into the body for the same reason. Through experimentation, Paracelsus found that opium could be completely dissolved in alcohol, a preparation that made it absorbable. Paracelsus created a mixture of opium in brandy that he named laudanum, literally "something to be praised." Originally, his concoction also contained strange ingredients such as crushed pearls, a medicinal plant called henbane, and frog spawn, components that consumers later found to be unnecessary. According to

Paracelsus created a mixture of opium and brandy, a very potent means of ingesting the narcotic.

Paracelsus, laudanum could be used to treat any disease that caused pain. He even boasted that with his new drug, patients who had been bedridden with pain were able to regain much of their former, active lives. Students reported that "indeed he proved that patients who seemed to be dead suddenly arose."[5]

Interest in laudanum surged, and the drink was popular as a medicine and for recreational use. Men of learning sang its praises. Robert Burton (1577–1640), English scholar, priest, teacher, and author of *Anatomy of Melancholy*, recommended the use of laudanum for insomniacs who are kept awake "by reason of their continual cares, fears, sorrows, dry brain (which) is a symptom that much crucifies melancholy men."[6]

In 1680 Thomas Sydenham, an English physician and apothecary, revised the recipe of Paracelsus and called the new formulation Sydenham's Laudanum. Containing opium, sherry wine, saffron, cinnamon, and cloves, Sydenham's recipe tasted significantly better, and cost less, than the original. Sydenham, an enthusiastic proponent of opium, wrote, "I cannot forebear mentioning with gratitude the goodness of the Supreme Being, who has supplied afflicted mankind with opiates for their relief; no other remedy being equally powerful to overcome a great number of diseases, or to eradicate them effectually."[7]

Opium and the Arts

During the 1700s and 1800s opium was generally looked on as a treatment and a cure, not a drug of addiction. In fact, at that time the word *addiction* had little or no meaning to most people. Vials containing opium were cheap and readily available. Even though some people considered it to be as unrespectable as alcohol, many others embraced the drug enthusiastically. One reason for opium's acceptance in some circles was the praise and support the drug received from several influential writers.

Thomas De Quincey (1785–1859) was one of the first Europeans to pen his thoughts about opium. In 1821 he wrote "Confessions of an English Opium-Eater" describing his experiences with opium, a drug he first consumed to treat toothache pain and later began to use recreationally. De Quincey explained that he often saved his supply for important events, like a trip to the opera, because it enhanced his senses, making the experience seem larger than life. He wrote,

> That my pains had vanished was now a trifle in my eyes. . . . Here was the secret of happiness, that which philosophers had disputed for so many ages, at once discovered; happiness might now be bought for a penny, carried in the waist coat pocket; portable ecstasies might be had corked up in a pint bottle; and peace of mind could be sent down by the mail.[8]

His writing popularized the drug and brought it to everyone's attention. His later work, *Miseries of Opium*, which detailed the agonies of addiction, was largely ignored.

Although a less vocal supporter of opium, Elizabeth Barrett Browning (1806–1861), an English poet, consumed laudanum most of her adult life. Historians disagree on her original reasons

Poet Elizabeth Barrett Browning used laudanum to treat a restless condition.

for trying laudanum, but most concur that her continued use was to treat her neurasthenia, or general discomfort, a common diagnosis among ladies of the Victorian era. When asked by her husband-to-be why she did not reduce or discontinue her laudanum use, she replied:

> It might strike you as strange that I who have no pain—no acute suffering to keep down from its angles—should need dope in any shape. But I have had restlessness until it made me almost mad; at one time I lost the power of sleeping quite—and even in the day, the continual aching sense of weakness has been intolerable—besides palpitation—as if one's life, instead of giving movement to the body, were imprisoned undiminished within it, and beating and fluttering impotently to get out, at all the doors and windows. So the medical people gave me opium . . . and ever since I have called it my amreeta draught [drink of the gods], my elixir—because the tranquilizing power has been wonderful.[9]

Opium influenced the work of another English poet, Samuel Taylor Coleridge (1772–1834), who was introduced to the drug as a child, probably to treat a fever. In 1800 he took up opium again, this time to relieve back and joint pain. Coleridge realized that he was an addict and sought medical help on several occasions. However, he never kicked the opium habit. Coleridge eventually claimed that the dreams and hallucinations opium provided were the basis for his success as an author. One classic example of Coleridge's opium-induced work is the 1798 poem "Kubla Khan." Taking a small dose of opium, Coleridge went to bed early one night. After hours of vivid dreams, he awoke and recorded as much of his dream as he could remember; the rest he composed in his conscious mind. Many have interpreted the "dome" envisioned in his dream to be a place of serenity and beauty, perhaps a refuge from his gloomy life.

> I would build that dome in air,
> That sunny dome, those caves of ice!
> And all who heard should see them there,
> And all should cry, Beware! Beware!
> His flashing eyes, his floating hair!
> Weave a circle round him thrice,
> And close your eyes with holy dread,
> For he on honey-dew hath fed,
> And drunk the milk of Paradise.[10]

Opium in Patent Medicines

Sydenham's formula marked the beginning of the patent medicine industry in England. By 1700 other pharmacists competed with Sydenham by creating their own opium elixirs. However, the small amount of opium being imported into the country limited sales for all retailers.

Growth of opium-based medicines took off after Thomas Dover developed Dover's Powder, a treatment for gout. Dover, a well-known sea captain, had rescued the real-life Robinson Crusoe in 1709. When his sailing career ended, Dover announced plans to spend the rest of his life healing people. But because he was already forty years old, he felt that he did not have time to go to medical school. The captain preferred to heal people with his opium elixir. His friendships with sailors who were active in the opium trade made it possible for him to get all the opium he needed. In a short while, Dover's Powder was one of the most commonly purchased self-remedies in England.

Dover's Powder was quickly followed by D.J. Collis Browne's Chlorodyne, developed as a treatment for cholera. The medicine survives today with modified ingredients. In its footsteps followed Godfrey's Cordial, one of several opium-based soothing baby syrups. Sales of this baby syrup were enormous. In 1862 a pharmacist in Nottingham estimated that he sold twelve thousand doses a week. Most were bought by poor women who had to work long hours and take care of children. Soothing syrups helped keep the children quiet. In poverty-stricken families, the syrups may have had an additional positive side effect: They suppressed hunger and therefore saved on food.

Opium in America

Opium traveled with settlers to the New World in the early 1600s. Immigrants to America carried poppy seeds with them to their new home. Once established, many grew their own fields of opium poppies, scraped the resin from the seedpods, and dissolved the gooey sap in whiskey to treat pains and coughs. They also used the small black seeds in breads or pastries, or ground them to produce cooking oil.

During the California gold rush (1849–1860), large numbers of Chinese immigrated to North America. These settlers from the Orient brought many of their customs with them, and established opium dens in their new home like those in China. Opium dens were quiet rooms where customers could buy and smoke opium

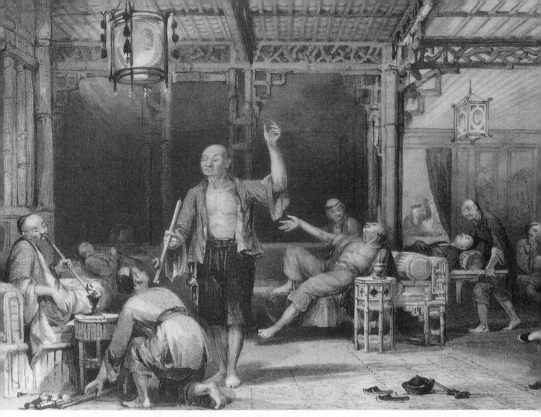

Chinese opium dens like this one thrived in America during the gold rush. Opium users bought and smoked opium in these quiet rooms.

under the watchful eye of the proprietor. For the first twenty years that the Chinese were in America, they were the only customers in the dens. Whites, viewing the dens with suspicion, did not enter. However, by 1868, American settlers began to smoke opium, much to the irritation of some local citizenry.

Many Americans feared opium smoking because they had heard rumors that it was dangerous. Even among those who appeared to make few moral judgments, opium smoking was considered to be a strange and sinful practice. For example, in 1877 the frontier town of Deadwood, South Dakota, was infamous in the Old West for its decadent nature. The settlement provided its citizens with every conceivable vice, including prostitution, drinking, and gambling. Yet, even in this tolerant setting, the sheriff was shocked to find members of the middle class smoking opium. In one investigation, he discovered small rooms furnished with cots holding "one, two, and sometimes four friends of both sexes, either dreaming off the effects of the deadly drugs, or else smoking."[11] Afraid of this new vice that would "quickly rob a (white) man of all semblance of man-hood,"[12] the sheriff closed all ten opium dens corrupting his city.

That same year, Winslow Anderson, a physician in San Francisco, recorded that, in his opinion, at least ten thousand local residents smoked opium. He said, "A large portion of the city had taken up smoking opium, hitting the pipe as often as three times a day." He was appalled to find girls "from sixteen to twenty years of age lying half-undressed on the floor or couches, smoking with their lovers."[13]

Some historians suggest that in the Old West, opium smoking was more common than alcohol consumption. Famous cowboys such as Kit Carson and Wild Bill Hickock were regular customers in opium dens. Although the Old West conjures up images of saloons full of cowboys, in reality, many cowboys were lying on cots

Opium's Advocate

In the July 1842 issue of the *Knickerbocker*, a New York magazine, writer William Blair described his experiences with opium.

> While I was sitting at tea, I felt a strange sensation, totally unlike any thing I had ever felt before; a gradual creeping thrill, which in a few minutes occupied every part of my body, lulling to sleep the before-mentioned racking pain, producing a pleasing glow from head to foot, and inducing a sensation of dreaming exhilaration (if the phrase be intelligible to others as it is to me) similar in nature but not in degree to the drowsiness caused by wine, though not inclining me to sleep; in fact far from it, that I longed to engage in some active exercise; to sing, dance, or leap . . . so vividly did I feel my vitality—for in this state of delicious exhilaration even mere excitement seemed absolute elysium [paradise]—that I could not resist the tendency to break out in the strangest vagaries, until my companions thought me deranged. . . . After I had been seated [at the play I was attending] a few minutes, the nature of the excitement changed, and a "waking sleep" succeeded. The actors on the stage vanished; the stage itself lost its reality; and before my entranced sight magnificent halls stretched out in endless succession with galley above galley, while the roof was blazing with gems, like stars whose rays alone illumined the whole building, which was tinged with strange, gigantic figures, like the wild possessors of lost globe. . . . I will not attempt farther to describe the magnificent vision which a little pill of "brown gum" had conjured up from the realm of ideal being. No words that I can command would do justice to its Titanian splendor and immensity.

in opium dens. Opium provided a novel way to pass the day away in a pleasant, pain-free stupor.

Despite all of the fears raised by open drug use in dens, opium was still valued in the Old West as well as the rest of the world because it could stop pain. Medicine was a young science and painkillers were scarce. Many accepted practices of the time seem almost barbaric by today's standards. Bloodletting, a common treatment for almost every illness, rarely helped and sometimes killed patients. Doctors did not wash their hands before treating patients because they were unaware that germs carry disease. Surgery, performed with unsterilized equipment on dirty tables,

American physicians in the Old West used opium as a painkiller, especially during surgeries like the one pictured.

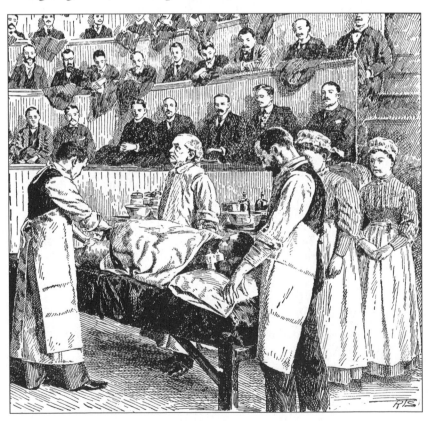

was an extremely dangerous procedure that often resulted in death. Any time a doctor could help patients avoid surgery by relieving pain, their chances of survival improved. For this reason, physicians referred to opium as "G.O.M." or "God's Own Medicine." For many years, opiates were prescribed freely and in good conscience to relieve pain and save lives.

The Power of Pain

Today pain is much better understood than it was in the nineteenth century. It begins when certain nerve cells, or neurons, are damaged or stimulated. However, pain is not perceived at the point of injury, but in the brain. The brain is a command center that coordinates the activities of the body's nerve cells and therefore the entire body. For example, if a child's hand touches a hot surface, she immediately jerks it away and cries. Her reaction is the result of orders given by her brain. When the hand contacted the surface, a series of events were set off. First, nerve cells were stimulated. These cells sent information to the brain, which quickly interpreted the messages. The brain then sent out a string of instructions that told her to move her hand, be aware of the damage to it, feel afraid, and cry out for help.

Messages travel to and from the brain along a pathway of nerve cells. The messages themselves exist in two forms: electrical and chemical. Electrical impulses originate within stimulated nerve cells. A stimulus to a nerve cell causes several changes to occur. First, tiny pores open, allowing charged particles to flow to the interior of the cell. Their presence upsets the balance of positive and negative charges that normally exists inside and outside the cell. In turn, this imbalance creates an electrical impulse. Like falling dominoes, the impulse moves from one point to the next, traveling down the length of the cell.

Once an impulse reaches the end of a cell, it moves to the next cell in the neuron path. However, no two nerve cells in the path actually touch one another. There is a gap, a little space called a synapse, between each neuron and the next cell. When an impulse reaches the end of a neuron, the electrical impulse cannot jump

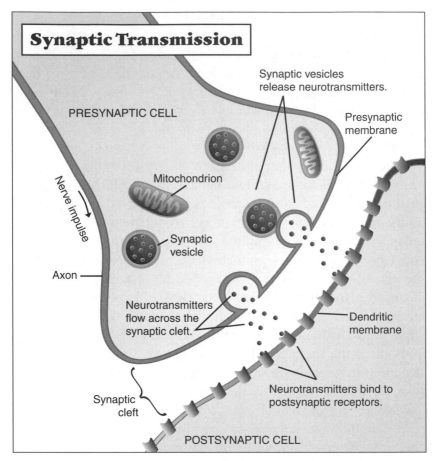

Synaptic Transmission

Synaptic vesicles release neurotransmitters.

PRESYNAPTIC CELL

Presynaptic membrane

Mitochondrion

Nerve impulse

Synaptic vesicle

Axon

Neurotransmitters flow across the synaptic cleft.

Dendritic membrane

Synaptic cleft

Neurotransmitters bind to postsynaptic receptors.

POSTSYNAPTIC CELL

across the synapse. Instead, chemical messengers called neuro-transmitters carry it over. On the far or postsynaptic side of the gap, special receptors provide a docking site for the neurotrans-mitters. The message continues down the line of neurons to the brain. The brain then sends a response message along another path of neurons back to the point of injury.

Chemicals That Block Pain

Any chemical that interferes with the transmission of a pain im-pulse stops the sensation of pain. The impulse can be blocked on its trip along nerves from the site of injury to the brain, or on the return trip from the brain back to the injury.

Different medicines block pain in different ways. Some slow the production of neurotransmitters, without neurotransmitters, the electrical impulse cannot get very far. Others block the receptors in synapses, preventing neurotransmitters from docking properly and stopping the conduction of the pain impulse.

In the mid-1900s, researchers began trying to understand exactly how narcotics block pain. In experiments, researchers mixed brain tissue with narcotics that had been tagged with radioactive materials. They found that brain tissue quickly attach to small amounts of opiates. Scientists knew from previous experiments that drugs get into cells in one of two ways: directly through the cell membrane, or by special receptors. This work had shown that those which travel through the membranes are generally required in large doses to be effective. On the other hand, drugs that are transported into cells by receptors are effective in much smaller amounts. Since brain tissue in the experiments only took up small quantities of tagged opiates, investigators suspected brain cells might have receptors for them. Solomon H. Snyder and Candace Pert, working at Johns Hopkins University School of Medicine, located these receptors in 1973.

Some areas of the nervous system have more opiate receptors than others. There are a lot of receptors in the part of the spinal cord that determines one's ability to tolerate pain. Snyder explains, "Opiates relieve pain at the spinal cord level by raising pain thresholds. Thus, if you were treated with morphine, an experimenter would have to administer a more painful stimulus than normal in order for you to notice any pain at all."[14]

Another part of the nervous system that has plenty of opiate receptors is the part of the brain that recognizes pain. Snyder says that

> the major analgesic activity of opiates is not so much a raising of the pain threshold as a blunting of the brain's subjective appreciation of pain. Patients who have been treated with morphine because of severe post-operative discomfort or extreme pain from cancer frequently tell their doctors, "It's a funny thing. The pain is still there, but it doesn't bother me."[15]

In short, when the brain stops worrying about the pain, the pain becomes more manageable.

The Body's Own Pain-Killers

After researchers Snyder and Pert found that the body possessed natural opiate receptors, they asked the next logical question: Since the body does not make opiates, why does the brain have special receptors for them? Scientists theorized that the body makes compounds that normally fit these receptors, and that these compounds have a chemical structure similar to that of opiates. Even before they were located, scientists named these natural chemicals "endorphins," short for "endogoneous morphine."

It is now known that endorphins, or enkephalins as some of them are called, are neurotransmitters released in response to deep pain. Endorphins are short-lived, natural chemicals that bind to the receptors then rapidly degrade. Because endorphins do not remain in brain cells for a long time, they have none of the unwanted effects of narcotics. For example, narcotics are addicting drugs, but endorphins do not have the ability to addict.

Endorphins play valuable roles in survival. When a person is in a dangerous situation, endorphins flood the body, preventing the perception of pain. This enables a person to escape from danger even if they have an injury. Runners and other athletes produce large amounts of endorphins when they push their bodies to their physical limits. Many athletes report that they never feel bad or suffer any pain until after a competition, when their endorphin levels begin to drop.

Marathon runners and other athletes produce large amounts of endorphins, compounds produced by the human body to temporarily block pain.

The euphoria produced by opiates can also be partially explained on a biochemical basis. In the brain, "several structures . . . are collectively referred to as the limbic system because they form a ring, or 'limbus,' surrounding the brainstem. A large body of research suggests that these structures are the major regulators of emotional behavior."[16] The presence of opiate receptors in the part of the brain that helps control emotions ties opium use to feelings of happiness.

Flower Power

Opium's extraordinary power to alter sensation is due to the close fit of opium molecules with the receptors in the human brain. Opium and its derivatives match structures in the brain like keys slipping into locks. Because of its ability to relieve pain and alter perception, opium has a long history of use in religious ceremonies, medical treatments, and recreational activities. The drug has been hailed as a gift from heaven, a kiss from the gods, and an instrument to raise the dead. However, its negative effects have become apparent over the years.

Chapter 2

Search for the Perfect Painkiller

As early as the sixteenth and seventeenth centuries, some physicians suspected that opium was addictive and that its continuous use was dangerous. In *The Mysteries of Opium Reveal'd*, a 1701 publication, Dr. John Jones of Oxford listed more than one hundred treatments that used opium. According to Jones, the drug relieved distress, anxiety, and a multitude of other health problems. However, he also pointed out that patients experienced pain if they suddenly stopped using the drug. "The effects of sudden leaving off the uses of opium after long and lavish use therefore [were] even great and intolerable distresses, anxieties and depressions of the spirit, which commonly end in a most miserable death, attended with strange agonies."[17] He went on to explain that by returning to their usual dose of opium, their agonizing symptoms quickly disappeared, a sure indicator of addiction.

Concerns about opium's addictive nature led scientists to study the compound more closely. Systematic investigation of opium began in 1805 with the work of German scientist, Friedrich Serturner. Serturner aimed to isolate opium's pain-relieving ingredient. Many others were on the same quest because the scientific community believed that the active ingredient alone would not be

30

addictive. Serturner's research showed that opium is a mixture of sugars, resins, waxes, water, and twenty different alkaloids, compounds that contain nitrogen. In his experiments, he found that one of these alkaloids had a dramatic effect on animals. He isolated this compound and called it morphine after Morpheus, the god of dreams, in keeping with the Greek tradition of naming drugs after deities. Serturner's work was a breakthrough in chemistry that earned him the Nobel Prize in 1831.

The isolation of morphine, coupled with the coincidental timing of another technical advance, changed the treatment of pain forever. In 1853 Alexander Wood invented the hypodermic syringe, a hollow tube with a needle on one end. The hypodermic needle made it possible to dissolve a drug in water and inject that solution directly into the body of a patient. This new drug delivery system, which was immediately applied to morphine, delighted physicians for several reasons. Because the digestive system was bypassed, the drug gave faster results. Since the amount of morphine included in an injection could be measured exactly, its

Named for the Greek god of dreams Morpheus (pictured), morphine is an addictive compound found in opium.

results were more reproducible than those gained by eating or drinking morphine elixirs. Also, doctors believed that injected drugs would help solve problems of addiction. In that day, scientists thought that drug addiction occurred in the stomach, and that one of the reasons opiates were addicting was because they were consumed.

On the Front Lines and at Home

Morphine and the hypodermic syringe were ready for use at the beginning of the American Civil War and the Franco-Prussian War. The administration of morphine on the battlefield was both a blessing and a curse for many of the wounded. The drug was meted out orally and by injection to help quell the pain of injuries and emergency surgery. It was also distributed liberally to hun-

This nineteenth-century poster advertises family medicines. Morphine was as readily available to the public as such medicines.

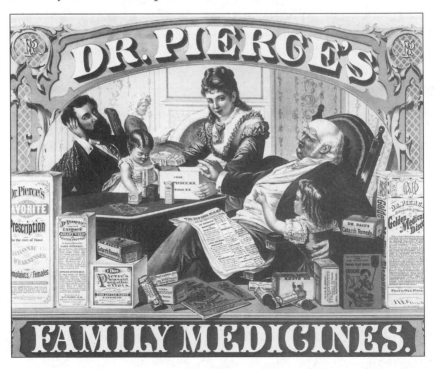

dreds of soldiers on a daily basis to treat dysentery and malaria. Historian Martin Booth explains how "Union Surgeon Major Nathan Mayer did not even dismount from his horse to dispense opium. He poured out what he termed 'exact doses' into his hands and let recipients lick it from his gloves."[18] In the long run, Serturner's wonder drug saddled hundreds of soldiers with a new problem, a lifetime addiction to morphine. After the Civil War morphine dependence was so common that it was called the "soldiers' disease."

Even though morphine addiction and its symptoms were gaining recognition, very few people fully understood its dangers. Therefore, morphine use continued to spread through the nineteenth century. In both Europe and the United States, many members of the middle class and high society injected the drug daily, either as a "cure" for opium addiction, to treat pain, or for the pleasurable feelings it gave. Stores and magazines openly sold morphine and syringes; syringe kits were even featured in the Sears catalog. It has been estimated that by the end of the century about one hundred thousand morphine addicts lived in the United States.

Most users began through medical use of the drug. Local pharmacies sold a variety of remedies that contained either morphine or opium. Paregoric, a mixture of opium and alcohol, was advertised as a treatment for babies with upset stomachs. Paregoric is one of the few early opium remedies still available today. Dozens of other stomach soothers and cough syrups were liberally supplemented with these powerful drugs. In the 1800s most medicines did not carry labels stating their ingredients, so consumers rarely knew what a prepared elixir contained. Even if they had known, few would have been alarmed to find opiates in their medications.

Many users preferred to drink morphine-laced beverages over alcoholic ones. In a paper titled "Advantages of Substituting the Morphia Habit for the Incurably Alcoholic," published by the Cincinnati Lancet-Clinic in 1898, physician J.R. Black claimed that morphine drinks were safer than alcohol. He stated that morphine

"calms in place of exciting the baser passion, and hence is less productive of acts of violence and crime; in short . . . the use of morphine in place of alcohol is but a choice of evils, and by far the
lesser." Black then pointed out the cost-effectiveness of morphine:

> On the score of economy the morphine habit is by far the better. The reg-
> ular whiskey drinker can be made content in his craving for stimulation, at
> least for quite a long time, on two or three grains of morphine a day, di-
> vided into appropriate portions, and given at regular intervals. If pur-
> chased by the drachm at fifty cents this will last him twenty days. Now it is
> safe to say that a like amount of spirits for the steady drinker cannot be
> purchased for two and one half cents a day, and that the majority of them
> spend five and ten times that sum a day as a regular thing.[19]

An Addict in the Home

In the late nineteenth century, it was considered unseemly for a
lady to drink alcohol; however, elixirs containing morphine were
not frowned upon. Many women used the drug to reduce tension and anxiety. As a result, the majority of morphine addicts
were white, middle-class women, a group of consumers who had
enough money to hire a doctor and to purchase the medicines he
prescribed.

Doctors probably knew less about the health of women than
they did about any other group of people. Conditions such as fa-
tigue, weakness, and anxiety were diagnosed as diseases that war-
ranted medical care. Morphine was the standard and accepted
treatment for these problems and many others, including the pain
of childbirth and complications caused by it. One morphine patient was Ella O'Neill, mother of playwright Eugene O'Neill. After the difficult delivery of Eugene in 1888, Mrs. O'Neill's doctor
prescribed the narcotic to treat her pain and to ease the depression
she was still feeling over the previous loss of an infant child.

Mrs. O'Neill fell prey to the grip of morphine, and lived as a
quiet, reclusive addict for the next twenty-five years. Eugene and
his siblings did not know why their mother was shy and sickly until, as young men, they happened upon her one day while she was
injecting her drug. Morphine addiction proved to be the source of
much unhappiness in the family. Ella's husband always hated the

Playwright Eugene O'Neill's mother began using morphine shortly after his birth and quickly became addicted.

poison that changed his happy wife into a thin, wasted shadow of her former self. Ella blamed the "cheap quack" that her husband hired, a doctor who was practicing standard medicine of the day. Ella sought help by going away for treatment again and again without success. She did not free herself from addiction until she entered a Brooklyn convent in 1914.

Just like Ella O'Neill, thousands of other patients and doctors found that the drug that had once looked like a long-sought magic potion, in reality caused another affliction. Problems with morphine addiction were brought to the public's attention when several addicts wrote about their suffering. In 1903 Reuben Blakey Eubank penned the tale of his addiction in *Twenty Years in Hell: The Life, Experience, Trials, and Tribulations of a Morphine Fiend*. Eubank explained how a stomach ailment started him on morphine: "With each recurring attack I would send for the doctor and have the morphine injection repeated. Never for a moment did I suspect that I was laying the foundation for a habit which I would carry with me to the grave. At first, habit only binds us with silken threads, but alas! Those threads finally change to links of strongest steel."[20]

A Heroic Drug

As doctors documented more and more cases of morphine addiction, their concerns grew. Eventually, the new drug's darker side could no longer be ignored. John Witherspoon, who later became president of the American Medical Association, begged the medical community to "save our people from the clutches of this hydra-headed monster which stalks abroad through the civilized world, wrecking lives and happy homes, filling our jails and lunatic asylums, and taking from these unfortunates, the precious promise of eternal life."[21]

Soon researchers turned back to the lab in pursuit of that elusive, nonaddicting painkiller. In 1874 experiments on morphine by English pharmacist C.R. Alder Wright yielded a derivative that is chemically known as diacetylmorphine. After testing the chemical on dogs, Wright found that it caused "great prostration, fear, sleepiness speedily following the administration and a slight tendency to vomiting."[22] Unimpressed with the chemical, he decided against any further research in morphine.

In 1897 more than twenty years after Wright's work, German scientists at Bayer Pharmaceutical Company reexamined his finding with a different perspective. Heinrich Dreser, head of the lab, realized the commercial possibilities of a morphine-related medication. He set out to test diacetylmorphine on a variety of animals, including fish, frogs, and rabbits. He even tested it on the workers at the Bayer plant. The drug provided them with instant pain relief along with an intense euphoria, followed by several hours of dreamy relaxation. They all loved it, and some reported that it made them feel empowered, strong, and "heroic."

By 1898 Bayer was manufacturing the chemical and promoting it as a treatment for coughing, bronchitis, and asthma as well as a cure for morphine addiction. Optimistically, Bayer claimed that the treatment had the painkilling properties of morphine but none of the troublesome addictive effects. This new wonder drug was dubbed heroin. Bayer sent samples to doctors all over the world and began an aggressive advertising program. By 1899 the company was producing a ton of heroin a year. Heroin became one of their most important products, making up 5 percent of Bayer's total drug sales. The majority of their heroin landed in the United States, where the drug was an immediate sensation.

Initially the American and international medical communities were as excited about the release of heroin as they had been about the development of morphine. In 1900 the *Boston Medical and Surgical Journal* praised the drug: "It possesses many advantages over morphine. It's not hypnotic and there's no danger of acquiring a habit."[23] Many doctors prescribed it to relieve constant, hacking coughs. In that day, doctors actively sought new ways to treat fatal respiratory diseases such as tuberculosis and pneumonia. Antibiotics held promise, but these drugs were relatively new and were not yet able to eliminate many deadly respiratory diseases.

Tuberculosis patients are treated outdoors with heroin to ease their painful coughing. Doctors were slow to discover the addictive nature of this narcotic.

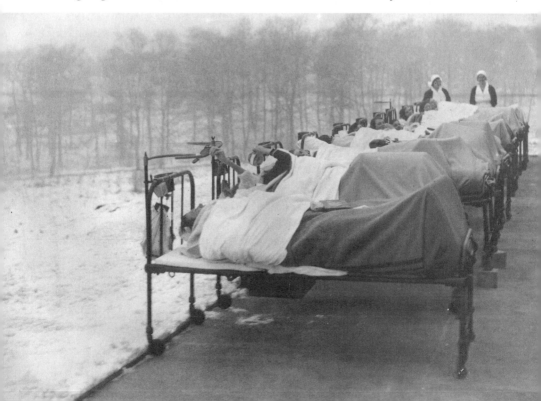

Heroin quickly became the drug of choice for patients suffering from incurable tuberculosis, and doctors prescribed it to hundreds of patients to stop their painful coughs.

Slowly, reports of scattered cases of heroin addiction trickled back to the medical community, and warnings began to appear in the literature. In 1903 Dr. George E. Pettey wrote "The Heroin Habit: Another Curse" in the *Alabama Medical Journal*, pointing out the dangers of heroin use. Pettey reported that in the last 150 cases he had treated for addiction, eight patients were addicted to heroin, and that three of the eight had become addicted during treatment by medical professionals.

Even so, some physicians did not readily believe the drug was dangerous. Across the country, medical practitioners continued to prescribe heroin. In 1911 John D. Trawick of Kentucky described the dilemma: "I feel that bringing charges against heroin is almost like questioning the fidelity of a good friend. I have used it with good results, and I have gotten some bad results, such as a peculiar bandlike feeling around the head, dizziness, etc., but in some cases referred to, it has been almost uniformly satisfactory."[24]

Many of the doctors who supported heroin as a valid medication were confused; the reports they read were in direct conflict with the results they saw in their own patients. The discrepancy was due to two factors. Most of these physicians prescribed heroin in pill form, which caused addiction so gradually that neither the doctors nor the patients noticed it. Also, scores of patients suffered from life-long health problems, so they never stopped taking the medicine, and therefore never suffered the withdrawal symptoms, the standard red flags that signal addiction.

In 1913 Bayer decided to stop making the wonder drug. The company had received hundreds of reports of hospital admissions for heroin overdoses in the United States. It was clear that heroin had a following of recreational users. A large group of habitual users had even been identified and nicknamed "junkies" because they raised money for their habits by collecting and selling junk metal.

Without Bayer as a source of drugs, many users turned to illegal markets. By 1925 it was impossible for anyone to ignore the warnings any longer. Researchers reported that in the United States there were more than two hundred thousand heroin addicts. The drug proved to be much more addicting than morphine. Eventually, the newest painkiller was banned from medical use in the United States.

Today scientists know more about heroin than Wright or Dreser could ever hope to learn. It is a powerful drug, even more potent than morphine. Heroin's potency is due to its ability to dissolve in fat. Since much of the tissue in the brain contains fat, heroin passes into cells of the brain faster than morphine. Therefore, it gives quicker, more dramatic results. Its power is clear in one young man's description: "After that first shot of heroin, I thought 'WOW, where have you been my whole life?, this is where it's at.' It gave me that false euphoric feeling I had never known before; it became my girlfriend, my God, my mother and my career."[25]

The Heroin Experience

When heroin hit the market as a medication, it quickly found its way into the hands of recreational users. Today it is still the most common illegal narcotic in the United States. Fortunately, heroin use among teens appears to be dropping. According to a survey conducted by Monitoring the Future, an ongoing study of values, behaviors, and attitudes in teens and young adults, the percentage of high schoolers who tried heroin dropped from 1 percent to 0.5 percent from 1975 to 1979. The number remained stable near 0.5 percent for fourteen years, then rose and peaked in 1997 at 1.6 percent of the high school population. Since that time, it has dropped again, stabilizing at about 0.9 percent in 2001.

Heroin's ability to create a state of euphoria makes it very attractive to recreational users. Trout, a young addict, recounts his first experience with heroin: "I snorted two of the packets and sat back to wait. Nirvana. And thus I knew that this was the Real Deal. Soon a feeling of primal well-being filled my body, like a warm, bubbly pink liquid. It was almost like . . . getting an expert massage, and then stepping into a hot tub. It was the epitome of 'Chill.'"[26]

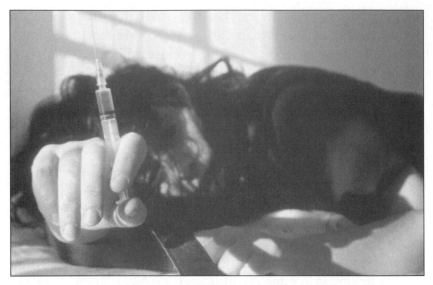

A heroin addict collapses after shooting up. In addition to feelings of euphoria, heroin users also suffer from nausea, vomiting, and dizziness.

However, first-time experiences with heroin are not always pleasant ones. The initial intravenous injection can cause nausea and vomiting, a distasteful event that is enough to keep some people from trying it again. However, many will give the drug another chance and soon a novice starts noticing the pleasant feelings or euphoria of heroin that are described as two experiences, a "rush" and a "high." The rush, which lasts only one or two minutes, feels like a great release of tension which pervades the whole body. After the rush, a warm, contented high lasts for four or five hours. Some users report a feeling of mild dizziness and a lack of interest in the people or activities around them. Sensations of hunger, pain, and anxiety disappear while heroin is in charge.

When Travis tried heroin for the first time, he felt both the rush and the high.

> The first time . . . I injected myself the onset was immediate and for about a minute I had an intense rush, it felt like your head blowing up or the entire world being torn apart. After that I got a pleasant warmness and intense feeling of relaxation. It was an effort to raise my eyelids. I could barely scratch my nose.

The feeling off smack [heroin] is like those sunny days when you go swimming and get out of the pool too let the sun dry you off but better. Its like coming in from a terrible cold day to get underneath the blankets and get that warm tingly sensation but better. . . . You don't care about anything. There's no euphoria just a pleasant feeling of nothingness.[27]

Still Seeking the Perfect Drug

Researchers have never given up hope of finding a nonaddictive painkiller. Since heroin's debut, scientists have designed countless other narcotic drugs. A few of these have proved reliable and have been adopted for use by the medical community along with their parent drug, morphine.

Physicians fully understand morphine's power as well as its dangers, so it is used more conservatively today than it was in the past. However, it remains an important drug in the treatment of pain and in situations associated with pain. Morphine can be given before surgery to relieve anxiety and reduce the amount of anesthetic required, then again after surgery to reduce pain. It is an excellent drug for treating severe pain that results from serious

Dope for Sale

In October 1996, interviews with addicts resulted in an essay, "Inside the Philadelphia Heroin Culture," describing some experiences in their lives:

> The heroin economy is extremely well developed in Philadelphia, as it is also in New York City. It has been in place for years and serves a large pool of addicts in the greater metropolitan area. With increased competition and the relatively recent abundance of cheap, pure heroin, the market has changed from one based on large profits for small amounts of high risk to one of large amounts at small profits and low risks. . . . Here, at places well known to purchasers, merchants staff sections of street, starting at 7 in the morning and working shifts until far into the night. They shout "Dope! Dope! Dope!" at cruising cars. Such solicitations are always blatant and can easily be denied should they result in a confrontation with authorities; the actual drugs are kept hidden around a corner. . . . The product comes sealed in clear cellophane and is stamped with a trademark identifying the product. Example trade names include "I'll be back," "Whitehouse," "Viper," "V*," "Fugitive," "Cowboy," "Gandy," and "Game of Death."

injury, cancer, or kidney stones. It is usually administered as an intramuscular injection, but can also be given orally.

Several other morphinelike drugs have been developed. Three of these, hydrocodone, meperidine, and fentanyl, are almost as effective as morphine in reducing pain. Hydrocodone, also known as Dilaudid or Vicodin, is the second-oldest synthetic narcotic. On the street, hydrocodone pills may be called

Doctors administer morphine during surgery. The drug is also used to treat serious injuries, cancer, and pain from kidney stones.

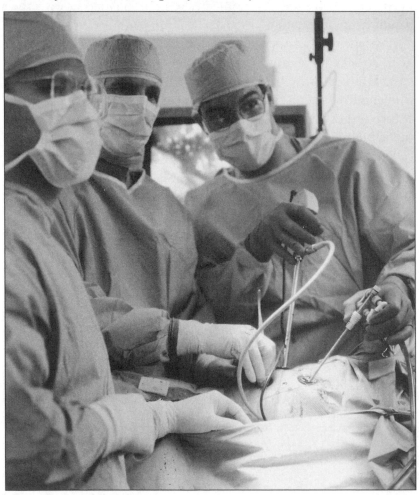

A Deadly Dose

Abuse of OxyContin has proved to be a death sentence for many naive users. In an interview, Serena Altschul of CBS's *48 Hours Investigates*, August 23, 2002, meets Summer Ulman and learns about the tragic death of Summer's sister, Shauna.

Summer was 14 when she began to hang out with 18-year-old Rufus Simpson. Shauna was 13. In late January, 2000, the sisters snuck out to a party at Simpson's house.

He offered them drugs. They had no idea they were taking OxyContin.

After Summer took the pills, she passed out. When she woke up she was woozy. She realized that Rufus was frantic, saying that Shauna was dead. Summer listened to her sister's heart, and heard nothing.

Toxicologist Bruce Goldberger . . . said that "The level of oxycodone in Shauna's blood was about the highest we've ever seen."

He estimates Shauna took six 80 milligram pills. "If I took an Oxy-Contin 80, there's a good chance I would die," he says. . . . "It packs this powerful punch."

Prosecutor Don Scaglione traced the OxyContin that killed Shauna back to a legitimate source, a woman who was dying of cancer. After she died, the pills . . . passed through the hands of several teens . . . who ended up at the party. Simpson pled guilty to manslaughter. He was sentenced to fifteen years.

Summer believes that Shauna's story needs to be told. "Everybody knows because of this girl that died, there's something out there that you need to watch out for," she says.

Dillies. The drug is often prescribed for terminally ill patients because it is very potent but has few of the undesirable side effects such as nausea.

Meperidine or Demerol, called Demmies on the street, is only one-sixth as strong as morphine. Since it can cause nausea and vomiting when taken orally, it is usually injected. One of the most widely used prescription analgesics, meperidine is effective for treating the pain of childbirth, as well as conditions such as migraine headaches.

Fentanyl, a pain reliever that is eighty times more potent than heroin, was first produced in the late 1950s. In the 1960s it gained popularity in hospitals as an intravenous anesthetic. Variations of fentanyl are still used in surgery to help put patients to sleep and in treatment of extreme pain. When used illicitly, it delivers a rush and several hours of high very much like heroin.

Several other synthetic narcotics have been modeled after morphine and are used to treat mild to moderate pain. Propoxyphene, also known as Darvon, and pentazocine, sold as Talwin, are reliable drugs for pain management. Another narcotic, methadone or Dolophine, can also be used to treat pain. However, it is most commonly used to treat addiction to more habit-forming narcotics like heroin.

Besides morphine, opium contains another alkaloid, codeine, although this compound is present in much smaller quantities. Even though codeine was originally isolated from the opium plant, most codeine used in medications today is made in the lab. Codeine is a widely prescribed painkiller. Each year in the United States, about 1.2 million pounds (55,000 kilograms) are made, enough for everyone in the country to have sixteen therapeutic doses. Codeine's action is similar to that of morphine, but at only one-seventh of the potency. Codeine is thought to be less addictive than morphine, so it is administered for mild to moderate pain and to relieve cough and diarrhea. For reasons that are not completely understood, codeine is ineffective for about 20 percent of the population.

Like morphine, codeine has been used as both a model and a parent for the creation of new drugs. Oxycodone is a narcotic that is synthesized from codeine. When mixed with aspirin it is sold as Percodan, and with acetaminophen it is called Percocet. Oxy-Contin tablets are a timed-release formulation of oxycodone. OxyContin contains a relatively high level of oxycodone, but it is designed to be released slowly throughout the entire day.

The Hunt Goes On

In a never ending quest to find the perfect painkiller, scientists have created a variety of drugs. Some of these have great medical value. However, all opium-like medications have a troublesome history of addiction.

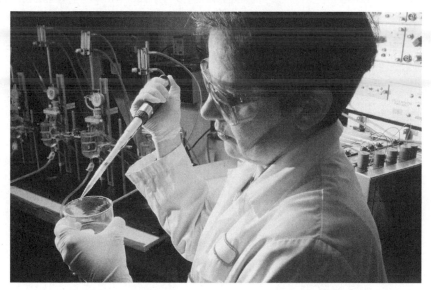

Scientists continue to search for a drug with the power of opium but without its addictive qualities. Drugs like morphine, heroin, and codeine are results of this search.

The development of morphine from opium released a powerfully addictive drug on the world. Heroin proved even more addictive. In the space of only one hundred years, science converted opium into a drug so powerful that hundreds of thousands of Americans spend their entire lives in its grip.

Chapter 3

Narcotic Addiction and Abuse

Americans, descendants of rebels and explorers, often push themselves to the edge in search for the ultimate challenge or reward. But in the never ending quest to experience it all, some have pushed too far. Those who have chosen to try narcotics for thrills have hitched their lives to the most addicting group of drugs in the world.

An addiction is a complex condition that results in an emotional and physical inability to avoid drug use. Eventually, an addict is compelled to continue taking the drug, even when met head-on with harmful consequences. Addiction affects a person's body as well as his or her mind.

Narcotics' chemical effects on the brain make them so addicting. Sections of the brain and spinal cord contain cells loaded with opiate receptors, structures that normally bind to the body's own painkilling chemicals. When these natural chemicals bind to the receptors, pain signals traveling to the brain are diminished. Because the physical structures of the natural chemicals are very similar to the structures of narcotics, narcotics are also capable of binding to cells' receptors for natural painkillers.

But once bound, narcotics do more than just block some of the pain. They also stimulate an area of the brain called the pleasure center, giving a rush of euphoria and several hours of blissful stupor. In some of the people who experiment with narcotics, these sensations feel better than anything they have experienced before.

The Price of Pleasure

The pleasures of narcotics are quickly clouded with problems. In a very short time, a user finds that the small dose that originally produced complete happiness is no longer effective. This change occurs because the presence of narcotics in the brain causes it to stop using its own built-in pain-blocking mechanisms. When these mechanisms break down, narcotics lose some of their effectiveness. As a result, the user needs increasingly larger doses of narcotic to experience the euphoria felt earlier on a much lower dose. This condition is called habituation or tolerance because it takes more of the drug to get high. Habituated users may take dangerously high doses of narcotics in an effort to re-create the pleasurable experiences they had earlier. Abusers taking large, frequent

An addict lies on a bed after using narcotics. Addictions affect the user's mind and body, creating a chemical dependency on the drug.

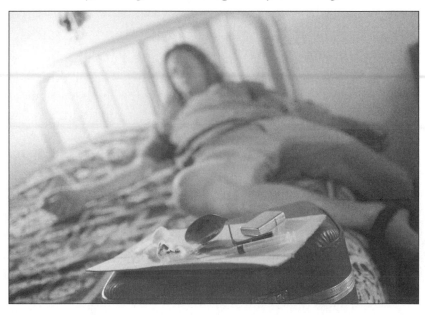

doses of narcotics find that their habits quickly become expensive, and when money is lacking, some turn to criminal acts to get cash. Some addicts steal from friends and family, commit robbery, or even prostitute themselves to support their habits.

A young heroin addict explains how her drug habit led her to steal from her family:

> I was 16 when I first snorted heroin. I was in my car and my cousin just happened to have some on him. I was like "Let me try, let me try," and he did. But he only gave me a very tiny amount, so it really didn't even do much.

> When I was 17 . . . (a boy had) heroin. I did the whole bag and I was really high. I threw up and all that, but it was great. It was just the most wonderful feeling. That's when it started and I was hooked until I was 21. I had no idea how addictive it was.

> Within three months, I was doing it every day. I was working at a car wash and I blew most of my money on the heroin. Then I started stealing from my parents. I wrote out checks of theirs to myself. I stole my mom's jewelry. I'd take anything around the house that was of value and pawn it off. I stole equipment from my little brother's band, and that's why his band broke up. I never tried prostitution or anything like that.[28]

Who Needs Help?

Concerned families, friends, and professionals want to help a person who is experimenting with narcotics. However, narcotic use is not always easy to identify. Even medical professionals have guidelines they follow to help them make a determination. One red flag is constricted pupils and sensitivity to light. The person may even appear intoxicated or sleepy. Teen Challenge, a source of help for young people dealing with heroin, says:

> When someone has had a sufficient dosage, or from an hour to two hours after injecting "smack" (heroin) he might "nod out" (literally fall in and out of a sleeping state) in the middle of a conversation or even while driving. Addicts refer to this as being "on the nod." It is not uncommon for heroin addicts to "nod out" while smoking a cigarette and subsequently suffer burns on their fingers where they were holding the cigarette. In the same way they often burn holes in their clothing or in the furniture where they are sitting or lying.[29]

A Day in the Life

John Patten, writing for *Packet Online,* interviewed a young narcotic addict and recorded his story.

> Each and every day, a 20-year-old East Windsor resident we'll call Kent wakes up with a mission—to go to Trenton and buy enough heroin to get through the day. It's a mission that has ruled his life for most of the last three years, and requires several hours each day. If he doesn't get the heroin, he will get sick before the sun goes down, convulsing in cold sweats.

> Kent said he was intrigued with the idea of trying heroin after watching movies like "Trainspotting" and "The Basketball Diaries." He remembers the Friday night in May 1997, when he snorted his first line of heroin and began a descent into the nightmare of heroin use.

> "The 'rush' was so good, I went back to it," he said.

> As Kent and his girlfriend continued their use—she was shooting up, while he snorted it—their tolerance to the drug grew. One tiny "bag" of heroin that cost $15 would get them both high once or twice when they started, but just two months later the same size bag would barely be enough to give him a "buzz." "Now, I need to do two bags in a . . . shot to get the same effect. If I want to get high, I need to use three bags."

> Now firmly in the clutches of the drug, Kent spends the better part of every day riding buses (his driver's license was suspended following a conviction for possession) to the "drug markets" in Trenton. After making his buy, he finds a public restroom—a donut shop or coffee shop—and shoots up. That's Kent's life, seven days a week.

> "The only thing this disease wants is to make you dead," Kent said. "Age, race and color don't matter—nobody is immune."

Once a drug user is identified, a medical professional may need to determine addiction. Whereas a narcotic abuser may use occasionally, an addict has developed a dependence on narcotics. Narcotic addiction should be suspected if an individual displays certain behaviors for a month or longer. For example, if someone starts missing important activities, such as participation in sports or attendance in school, addiction should be suspected. One telltale sign that differentiates addiction from abuse is the need for increasingly larger doses of the drug, or continued use over a longer period of time than originally intended. For example, a person who had planned to try a narcotic only one time may find that they keep coming back to the drug again and again. The inability to cut down on the amount of drug being used, a sign of habituation, is also an indicator.

Another symptom of addiction is continued use of the drug despite the knowledge that it will cause negative consequences, such as a conflict with the family or poor grades. While admitting that narcotics have caused her numerous problems, one woman says she continues to use them. She explains, "The first opiate I ever took was codeine. . . . It made me feel right for the first time in my life. Codeine was a revelation, and I've been an opiate user ever since. . . . Opiates have caused me lots of trouble."[30]

Withdrawal Syndrome: "Getting Sick"

Once a person's body has become habituated to narcotics, it is very difficult to stop using the drugs. Without the narcotic, the user experiences an unpleasant condition called withdrawal or "getting sick." Withdrawal, which has both physical and psychological components, refers to a set of symptoms that oc-

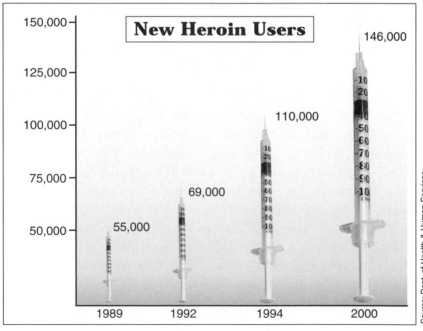

New Heroin Users

150,000
146,000
125,000
110,000
100,000
75,000
69,000
55,000
50,000

1989   1992   1994   2000

Source: Dept. of Health & Human Services.

cur after a person stops using an addictive drug. Withdrawal symptoms usually appear four to six hours after the last dose. Initial physical symptoms vary from one person to the next, but in many people they mimic a bad case of the flu, and include muscle aches, tearing of the eyes, runny nose, sweating, and yawning. Early psychological symptoms vary, but include anxiety and jitters.

Within twelve to fourteen hours, the symptoms begin to change from flulike to more severe. The pupils of the eyes become dilated, appetite diminishes, tremors pass through the body, aches get worse, and gooseflesh appears. This gooseflesh, normally associated with the feeling of being cold, may be the origin of the term *cold turkey* which is used to describe the sudden cessation of drug use. Feelings of sadness and depression may occur along with anxiety.

After fourteen hours, the addict feels tired and irritable. Insomnia, weakness, nausea, vomiting, chills, and muscle aches and spasms may still be present. Muscle spasms in the legs are believed to have led to the term *kick the habit*, which refers to the act of getting off of drugs. These withdrawal symptoms can persist for seven to ten days. Eventually these acute symptoms subside, and the addict moves into a phase of extended abstinence that causes a mild increase in blood pressure, body temperature, and respiration, as well as feelings of sadness and mild anxiety. Even after thirty weeks or more, the addict may still be experiencing some of these physical symptoms.

The symptoms of withdrawal are due to the lack of normal painkilling chemicals in the brain. Without these chemicals, it is impossible to experience relaxation, pleasure, or contentment. The brain does not start remaking its normal chemicals for several weeks or even months after drug use has ended. That explains why the addict feels sadness, pain, misery, and loneliness for so long. Nothing is interesting or entertaining, nothing feels or tastes good, and nothing brings pleasure. At this low point, the only way an addict can experience pleasure is through heroin, and the desire for the drug is strong.

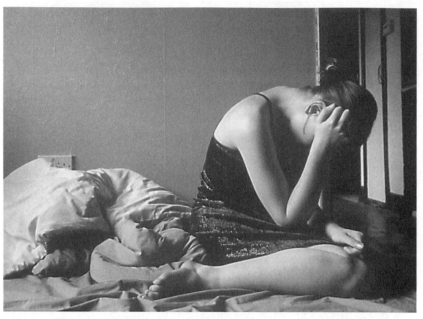

A girl suffers from depression, a common symptom of withdrawal.
Withdrawal results from a lack of addictive painkilling chemicals in
the brain.

A heroin addict describes his withdrawal experience to a friend
who is considering trying heroin:

> First thing that hits is an almost incessant yawning, and watery eyes . . . some
> flu like sniffles, maybe sneezing . . . then sweats and chills chills . . . lotsa
> chills. . . . But this is nothing . . . just a little prelude of the fun to come. . . .

> You basically feel like you want to die for the first three days, you throw
> up, your bowels ache and burn. . . . Muscle's ache . . . lower back knots.

> Severe detoxing of opioids, one may have uncontrollable shaking of the legs
> and thrashing due to severe anxiety . . . and cramping. . . . Sleep is impossible
> at first no position is comfortable, minutes seems like hours . . . anxiety con-
> sumes you . . . and you want to scream. . . . Panic, consumes you. . . .

> Long Hot Showers (saviors) in the middle of the night give minor relief . . .
> but that minor relief seems at that second like it is all that is keeping you
> alive . . . and so you really appreciate it and you want to remember all of it
> . . . so that you do not do it again. . . .

Sleep is Painful for a long while & after. . . . You have unbelievable nightmares . . . that stuns you with their impact on your psyche . . . and . . . endless headaches at this point . . . deep in your brain it seems. . . . Tylenol helps. . . .

What it is like to be very hungry and think of food . . . your mouth salivates for food, a conditioned response . . . heroin also conditions responses in you. . . . It simply becomes part of you. . . . It is an appetite you have now . . . and anything can set it off.[31]

Popular Drugs

As painful as withdrawal can be, it is not the most dangerous aspect of illegal narcotic use. Emergency room visits resulting from heroin overdoses have been increasingly common. In one Washington community, the number of opiate-related deaths increased by 140 percent between 1990 and 1999, the last year for which statistics are available. During the same time period, the community's population grew by only 11 percent. Opiate-related deaths occurred primarily in men between the ages of twenty-five and fifty-four.

High Quality, Low Prices

The U.S. Drug Enforcement Administration keeps track of drug use and the status of drugs across the United States. In 2001, the most recent year for which statistics are available, it reported that heroin is still one of the two "primary drugs of abuse in the state of Massachusetts. . . . High-quality heroin is available from gram to kilogram quantities throughout the state. . . . High-quality heroin is purchased in pure form, then cut [mixed with other ingredients] and repackaged for resale. Heroin distribution and use continues to be spread throughout the state, with extremely low wholesale/retail prices and purity levels routinely exceeding 60%. Abuse remains widespread, with continued reports of heroin overdose deaths and incidences occurring throughout the state."

The story is similar in other states. In California, the heroin is of very good quality and is smuggled into the state via Mexico. DEA agents explain: "The increased availability of high-purity heroin, which can effectively be snorted, has given rise to a new, younger user population. While avoiding the stigma of needle use, this group is ingesting larger quantities of the drug and, according to drug treatment specialists, progressing more quickly toward addiction."

In 2001 DAWN, the Drug Abuse Warning Network, surveyed emergency departments in cities across the United States. Although patterns of illegal drug use vary greatly from one city to another, their research showed that heroin is the second most commonly reported drug in Emergency Departments, accounting for forty-four out of every one hundred thousand visits. One city in particular, Detroit, has experienced an increase in heroin overdoses. The Community Epidemiology Work Group, a network of researchers from twenty metropolitan areas who follow trends in drug use, states in December 2001 that reports of heroin by emergency room doctors "has increased significantly in seven cities, including Detroit. . . . Heroin was responsible for 32 percent of drug-related admissions in Detroit hospitals, nearly half of all admissions statewide."[32]

A Dangerous Habit

People who are addicted to narcotics and many other drugs suffer long-term health problems. Users tend to be so focused on their drug they forget to take care of themselves. Consequently, they often eat poorly and lose weight. They also suffer from long-term constipation. Since opiates cause slow, shallow breathing, addicts do not take in enough oxygen to maintain normal levels in their blood. They experience long periods of hypoxia, or low oxygen. In the brain, lack of adequate oxygen can cause irreversible damage to neurons.

Heroin users who inject the drug face even more risks. Long-term abuse by injection can lead to scarred or collapsed veins and infections of blood vessels and the skin. Sharing injection paraphernalia has serious consequences because needles are an easy way to spread diseases carried in the blood. If a person who has a bloodborne disease shares a needle with someone else, the disease can be passed along to the second user. Diseases carried in the blood such as hepatitis C and AIDS can destroy a user's health. Intravenous drug use is responsible for one-third of all new cases of AIDS and one-half of new cases of hepatitis C in the United States. Once these conditions are contracted, they can then be passed on to sexual partners and to children.

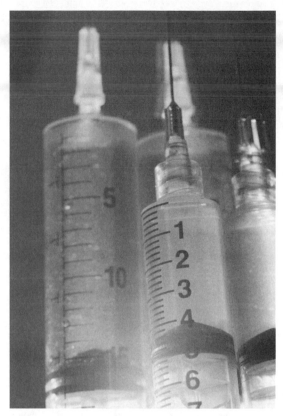

Syringes like these are used to inject heroin into the body. Long-term injection is very dangerous.

Heroin addicts also face danger because it is impossible for them to know the ingredients in their product. The quality of legal drugs is monitored by the Food and Drug Administration. However, illegal drug dealers make no promises about content or quality. As a result, users have no idea what kind of contaminants the heroin will contain, and they never know how much pure heroin they are getting in a purchase.

Heroin is prepared in unsupervised labs, then sold and resold by several different retailers. Each seller dilutes or "cuts" the drug to increase their profits. Any white powder can be used to dilute the original batch. Dry milk, talc, starch, and sugar work well, as well as poisons like strychnine. Strychnine causes the heart rate to increase, a response that naive purchasers may attribute to the heroin. Any contaminant poses problems when dissolved with the heroin and injected into the body. Some clog blood vessels while others damage vital organs like the liver or kidneys. Contaminants in heroin that damage the body are referred to as "bad dope."

On Monday, a customer may buy a packet of heroin that is only 10 percent heroin; 90 percent of it is starch. However, on Tuesday the same customer might purchase heroin that is 30 percent pure. Simply by snorting the same quantity on these two occasions, the user unwittingly gets a much stronger dose on Tuesday than on Monday. Large doses of heroin cause the respiratory sys-

Drugs can be purchased in an opium room like this one. Because dealers dilute their narcotics, users can never be sure of the ingredients used in their products.

tem to stop; as a result, the user quits breathing. About 1 percent of heroin addicts die each year from accidental overdose.

The purity of today's heroin poses another problem. Currently, heroin on the streets is the purest it has ever been, averaging about 40 percent. It is so pure that it does not have to be injected: It can produce a high and a rush by being sniffed or smoked. Without the stigma of the needle, heroin appeals to a larger group of people than ever before. A Worcester, Massachusetts, newspaper reports that the emergency room there sees a lot of heroin overdoses. "A lot more heroin users are snorting the drug as opposed to injecting it. When heroin is very pure and snorted, it causes a bad reaction. . . . many users are not accustomed to the pure heroin sold on the streets. . . . Users who get out of jail after a short hiatus from the drug are in for a surprise."[33]

For these reasons, overdoses can happen to novices or longtime heroin users. Will, an addict, tells about the death of his friend Harry from an overdose of heroin:

> Feeling fine, partying on, and as usual, talking the sort of crap to each other that only a 15 year friendship brings. We had the dope, and I nodded off. I woke up and Tom was dead. I knew as soon as I saw his grey face that this was true, but I'd revived him in the past, so I tried to now. It didn't work. The ambulance confirmed it. I remember giving him mouth-to-mouth and hearing a gurgling in his lungs.
>
> Why I'm still alive, I don't know, or only God knows, if you prefer. I can't say I would never take those drugs, if I had the time again, but I would do anything to bring Tom back, only I can't.[34]

Risks to Babies Born of Addicted Mothers

In addition to harming the user, narcotic use during pregnancy exposes an unborn baby to many additional risks. Any opiates ingested by the mother also enter the baby's bloodstream. As a result, babies of narcotic users are at higher than normal risks of problems. The most commonly reported complication is lower-than-normal birth weight. Other dangers are risk of death in the uterus, spontaneous abortion, and death during or shortly after delivery.

Narcotic use during pregnancy exposes babies to the drugs through the uterus.

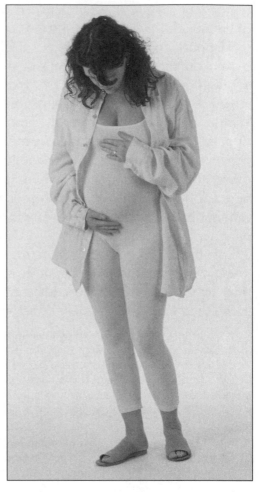

Babies who are exposed to high levels of narcotics in the uterus develop a physical dependence on them. Therefore, babies born to narcotic addicts are addicted at birth. As a result, they undergo withdrawal symptoms for several days. A baby in withdrawal is very irritable and has a high-pitched cry and tremors. It breathes faster than normal, sweats, vomits, and may experience diarrhea, fever, and seizures.

The experience of caring for an addicted infant can be heart-breaking. In an interview with a young addict, a reporter reveals some of the complications of narcotic use during pregnancy.

Marie gave birth to her first child just a week ago. But when the 29-year-old mother went home two days later . . . she had to leave her new daughter behind.

Like her mother, the infant is addicted to opiates.

. . . Marie passed her drug habit on to the child in her womb and now medical staff must care for the baby as it goes through the painful throes of withdrawal.

A Lifetime of Addiction

In the Schaffer Drug Library's *Consumer's Union Report on Licit and Illicit Drugs* written in 1972, Edward M. Brecher reviews some of the historical evidence supporting claims of an eminent surgeon's morphine addiction. William Stewart Halsted (1852–1922), known as the father of modern surgery, was one of the founders of the Johns Hopkins medical center. At his death at the age of seventy, he was honored for his many contributions to medicine. Halsted was surgeon in chief of Johns Hopkins University School of Medicine. In that position, he pioneered a breakthrough operation for breast cancer, the mastectomy. His keen insight into the need for good hygiene and sterile conditions in the operating room brought about the use of rubber gloves in hospitals. Halsted also developed an improved technique for blood transfusion. His creation of the Halsted School of Surgery still provides residents with the training they need to become surgeons.

Yet, decades after his death, it was revealed that the doctor suffered from addiction to morphine for much of his adult life. Halsted's addiction had so little effect on his work that he was able to keep it a secret. His problems probably began just like those of countless others who were following the correct medical protocol of his day for using morphine. At one time, this innovative surgeon was suffering from an addiction to cocaine, a highly stimulating drug. Morphine was advertised as a safe, nonaddictive drug that could be used to treat addiction to other drugs. Halsted tried it, and successfully weaned himself off of cocaine. However, he was never able to escape his daily fix of morphine.

Halsted's addiction, which would be scandalous by today's standards, was very understandable in his time. It was not uncommon for medical professionals to experiment on themselves with new drugs when they were introduced to the market. In the process of educating himself about medications that might benefit his patients, he learned firsthand about the addictive powers of the opiates.

The little girl cries more than most normal babies, a high-pitched fretful wail. She has trouble sleeping and gets the sweats. Sometimes when Marie pulls at her daughter's tiny hands, they remain clenched and rigid—a typical symptom of an addicted infant.

Initially, nurses will give the baby increasing doses of drugs, such as [a solution] of opium, to lessen the physical impact of withdrawal. Then they will slowly reduce the level of drugs until her small body has been weaned. The process could take two months.[35]

To prevent some of these problems, an addicted mother can switch to a drug called methadone during her last six weeks of pregnancy. Once on methadone, she can reduce her drug intake each day. By lowering narcotics levels in her own blood, a mother also lowers them in the fetal blood. Babies born with very low levels of narcotics suffer much fewer problems than those born with high levels.

The problems that opiates pose to individuals, their families, and their friends are life changing. Doctors agree that the only sure way to avoid opiate addiction is to never try narcotics. However, help is available to anyone who needs it, no matter how serious their addiction.

 **Chapter 4**

Treatment of Narcotic Addiction

Nearly all narcotic addicts believe that they can stop using drugs any time they choose. As Zeina, a twenty-one-year old heroin addict asserts, "Rehabs r useless. . . . I don't need a rehab i know I can do it myself."[36]

However, very few can break free from their addiction without help. Most long-term narcotic use causes changes in the brain that stay even after drug use has ended. These changes affect behavior, often compelling the addicts to use drugs even in the face of harmful consequences. Therefore, the addicts who are most successful at dropping their drug habits are those who enroll in a supervised treatment or rehabilitation program.

The First Step Is Detox

Regardless of which treatment program an addict uses, detoxification is the first step. Detoxification is the elimination of the drug from the addict's body, a move that in the long run helps reduce the cravings for more of the drug. The process is difficult because it causes withdrawal symptoms as soon as an addict's last dose of narcotics has been metabolized. Although rarely life threatening, withdrawal can be so physically painful and emotionally exhausting

61

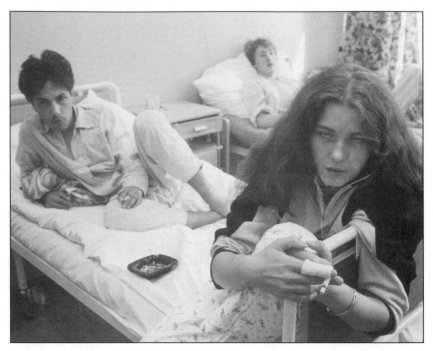

Patients suffer through withdrawal in a heroin detoxification center.
Detox is the first step in drug treatment programs.

that many addicts return to drug use just to end it. Therefore, detoxification is best accomplished in a setting that provides medical supervision and emotional support.

A few people are able to simply stop using narcotics, or go "cold turkey." However, this method is uncomfortable and few addicts endure it. Most undergo a supervised detoxification process in one of two ways: without the assistance of medication or with it. Those who do not use medication gradually reduce the size of their dosage over a period of time. Eventually, they quit taking the drug. Addicts who find this process to be too slow or difficult may choose to have the assistance of medication.

Roadblocks

One type of medication used in detoxification flushes the narcotic out of the addict's body. It works by occupying the opiate receptors in the brain and spinal cord, displacing the narcotics at their binding sites. Such chemicals, called opioid antagonists, are similar in structure to narcotics. Unlike narcotics, these medications are not drugs of abuse. They do not stimulate the cells they bind to, so they are not capable of causing a high or relieving pain.

Opioid antagonists are able to remove narcotics from their binding sites because they are more strongly attracted to opiate receptors than narcotics. Consequently, if heroin and an opioid antagonist are both present, the antagonist will bind to the receptor, leaving the heroin without a point of attachment. As a result, heroin has no effect on the cells.

As soon as a doctor administers an opioid antagonist to an addict, the patient begins to experience the discomfort of withdrawal. Withdrawal can be a tough experience. As one addict remembers, "Withdrawal from opiates is not life threatening—but it is an utterly miserable experience. You only feel like you're going to die."[37] To ease the process, the patient can be given other medications that help reduce pain and anxiety. Many patients remain under a doctor's care until withdrawal has passed, a matter of days or weeks, depending on the patient.

A commonly used opioid antagonist is Narcan. It cannot be absorbed from the digestive tract, so it is administered by injection. Since its effects last for only fifteen to thirty minutes, it must be administered repeatedly. Naltrexone, or Trexan, is similar to Narcan but it can be given orally, and its effects last much longer.

In a new procedure, some doctors put patients through a rapid detox. Ordinarily, a quick detox from narcotics would be unbearably painful. But in the new procedure, patients are kept under anesthesia while their bodies go through the worst stages of withdrawal. Naltrexone is given intravenously while the addict remains in an anesthesia-induced sleep for four to six hours. The advantage of rapid detox is that patients go through the worst stages of withdrawal, which include nausea, vomiting, cramps, and chills, while asleep. After rapid detox, residual amounts of narcotics remain in the blood for several days. If these rebind to the receptors, addiction will occur again, making the entire

No Pain

After interviewing the Green Bay Packers' quarterback Brett Favre in May 1996, Peter King wrote about Favre's drug addiction in "Bitter Pill." The article was reprinted in *The Reference Shelf, Substance Abuse*, a compilation of articles on drug abuse. In the interview, King learned about the events that led to Favre's abuse of narcotics and his subsequent treatment.

In May of 1996, Brett Favre knew he had a drug problem. One minute Favre was talking to his girlfriend Deanna Tynes, and the next he was lying in a hospital bed with tubes running out of his nose. Team physician John Gray leaned over his bed and said "You've just suffered a seizure, Brett. People can die from those." Favre knew his seizure was related to his addiction to narcotic pain-killers. He was finally ready to get help at the Menninger Clinic, a drug-rehabilitation facility in Kansas.

Favre, a football prodigy, quickly earned a reputation as a tough guy in football. However, this reputation was expensive. Between 1990 and 1996 Favre had five operations. Pain became a way of life for him. By 1995, Favre's old injuries were so painful that he started using Vicodin, a narcotic pain-killer, regularly.

Deanna had suspected Brett's drug problem for years. . . . Despite Deanna's pleas to get help, Brett felt sure that he could control his drug use and stay in the game. But the seizure got his attention, and he finally realized that he needed help.

Brett says, "People look at me and say, 'I'd love to be that guy.' But if they knew what it took to be that guy, they wouldn't love to be him, I can guarantee you that. I'm entering a treatment center tomorrow. Would they love that?"

After drug rehabilitation, Favre returned to the game he loves. Since 1996, the quarterback has admitted to, and dealt with, his narcotic addiction, putting him back on the road to glory.

Quarterback Brett Favre overcame an addiction to Vicodin, a narcotic painkiller.

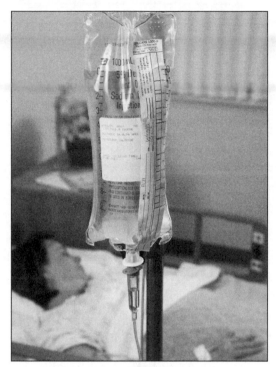

An IV can be used to administer detoxification medicine to a sleeping patient.

detoxing process futile. For this reason, the addict continues to take naltrexone for a few days to prevent relapse. Naltrexone also insures that if narcotics are used after treatment, the addict will not get high.

David Costello describes the experience of one young lady in rapid detox:

> Lisa Hill, a 27-year-old prescription drug addict, lies in a hospital bed in Tustin, about to undergo her third detox attempt. A few minutes later, doctors give her anesthesia, stick a breathing tube down her throat and then administer a liquid dose of Naltrexone. During the next few hours, the drug cleans Hill's body and brain of any remnants of the painkiller Vicodin that she has been hooked on since a car accident in 2000.
>
> If Hill were awake, she'd be suffering hours of severe headaches, vomiting, shakes, sweats and relentless abdominal pain. The doctors, though, don't wake her for several hours, and later give her sleeping pills to make it through the night. In the morning, she wakes up, takes a shower and goes home. A few hours later, she no longer craves.[38]

The treatment takes two days, from start to finish. "This is more successful than traditional treatments. And it's more humane," says Clare Waismann, director of the Waismann Institute in Beverly Hills, who brought the treatment to the U.S. five years ago from Israel, a major center of research into rapid detox programs. The number of patients undergoing treatment at the institute's clinic in Tustin has tripled in the last two years, Waismann says.

Rapid detox has its critics. Some physicians feel that it is dangerous for patients to remain under anesthesia for several hours. Others point out that it does not really matter how addicts detox; their success at beating drugs depends more on their ability to stick with a recovery program than on how they get the drugs out of their body. There are several recovery programs from which addicts can choose.

Methadone Treatment

Some of the oldest recovery programs for narcotic addiction are based on "harm reduction" approaches. The goal of all harm re-

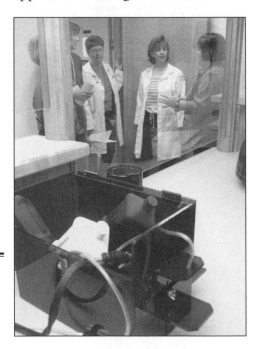

Pictured is a methodone distribution machine. Some clinics use this narcotic to wean addicts from heroin or morphine.

duction plans is to change an addict's lifestyle so that it is safer and enables the addict to function in society. Methadone treatment was the first harm reduction program, and it is still in use today.

In methadone treatment, a less problematic narcotic is substituted for heroin or morphine. Methadone affects the body differently than narcotics of abuse. It binds to opiate receptors in the nervous system, stopping the painful withdrawal symptoms and the strong craving for other drugs. However, at the doses given in treatment programs, it does not produce sedation or intoxication. Addicts on methadone treatment can drive their cars, keep jobs, and participate in family duties. Unlike heroin, whose effects wear off in about four hours, methadone lasts about twenty-four hours; therefore, addicts just need to visit the clinic once a day to get their medication. This is an important aspect of the program for people who work or take care of children. Methadone can be taken orally, which is a benefit to those who need to get away from the habit of injecting a drug. Some individuals use methadone instead of heroin or morphine while they wean themselves off of narcotics. Others maintain a narcotic addiction by taking methadone for years, a program called methadone maintenance.

Chris, a twenty-three-year old, discusses his narcotic addiction and the results of his methadone maintenance program:

> I've been doing heroin regularly since I was 17 or 18 . . . it didn't take long for me to lose everything I ever thought was valuable to me. . . . I lost my job, got kicked out of my folks house and then out of the friends house I moved into first. . . . i talked to my dad and told him I had had enough and I wanted to try the methadone program again, I had tried methadone before for a short time but just wasn't ready. . . . i've been on the methadone program for a year now. . . . I've had a job for a year and a place to live . . . i have the love and respect of my family and friends and self respect.[39]

Since methadone programs have been useful for many addicts, research for an even better substitute narcotic has been ongoing. LAAM, which stands for levoalphaacetylmethadol, is a newer medication that can prevent withdrawal and drug cravings for seventy-two hours. Therefore, patients need only report to clinics two or three times a week. This helps remove them one step farther from their associations with other abusers and gives them more

Chemistry Can Help

In "Treatment Offers Same Results, Fewer Side Effects" (December 10, 2002), *NBC News* carried the story of the newest chemical break-through for narcotic addicts. Praised as easy to use, the new drug, buprenorphine, holds a lot of potential. A recovering addict,

> [Otis] Rivers is now trying to get the word out about buprenorphine. Rivers joined a panel of experts from the Department of Health and Human Services and the U.S. Drug Enforcement Administration to un-veil the new medical treatment for people addicted to opiates such as heroin, and prescription painkillers like oxycontin and vicodin.

> Methadone, a painkiller, is the standard drug for treating opiate ad-diction right now, and has been for many years.

> Dr. George Kolodner, the director of Chemical Dependence at George-town University Hospital, said buprenorphine, an analgesic, is a big improvement.

> "It's just as effective as methadone in relieving the withdrawal symp-toms of whatever drug the person is using. But unlike methadone, the withdrawal symptoms from buprenorphine are relatively minor," Kolodner said.

> "There are people who are on painkillers and they want to go off painkillers and they are not quite sure what to do about that. To go to a specialized methadone clinic is sometimes a fairly protracted [drawn out] situation, where if they just go to their doctors it would be easier for them to get off," Kolodner said.

> Rivers said buprenorphine gave him a new life. Today, he hopes this new program will help thousands of people fight their drug addictions.

freedom in their lives. Buprenorphine, a newer release, is similar to methadone and LAAM, but has even fewer narcotic effects than either. It is hoped that buprenorphine will be especially use-ful in lowering a patient's physical dependence on narcotics.

The Controversial Side

Even though methadone, LAAM, and buprenorphine programs are accepted treatment plans for narcotic addiction, not everyone finds them satisfactory. Many feel that the only real treatment for narcotic addiction is total abstinence, and that substituting methadone for heroin or morphine is just swapping one narcotic for another. Some believe that maintenance does not address the addict's real problems. In their book *From Chocolate to Morphine*, authors Andrew Weil and Winifred Rosen explain the shortcomings of the methadone program.

> The main advantage of methadone maintenance is that it is better than leading a criminal life. The real problem with it is that it doesn't go to the root of addiction. Nor does it show heroin users how to get high in any natural, less restricting ways. It offers them no help with the problems that led them to abuse heroin in the first place. All it does is substitute one narcotic for another; the addict remains an addict, albeit in a less destructive way.[40]

Like other narcotics, methadone and its relatives lead to physical dependency. One strong argument against them is that addicts who want to be completely free of narcotics find withdrawal to be as, or even more, difficult as withdrawal from the original drug of abuse.

One veteran addict describes how hard it is to get off of methadone:

> I've been on both ends of withdrawals, heroin and methadone, every patient of methadone will always tell you the same, as I do; I can kick heroin anytime, but methadone that is something else. In 15 years of heroin addiction, I've kicked three times, "cold turkey." In 10 years of methadone,

An addict drinks methadone to treat his addiction. Because methadone can become as addictive as heroin, using the drug for treatment is controversial.

I've never kicked methadone. Once I landed in jail, I had to do 72 hours of jail time before I got to see the judge. I was literally on the floor screaming my guts out. About 12 hours before I was to see the judge, I demanded to be taken to a hospital, I just couldn't take it. I was cuffed, and looking like "chair" was glued to my back, I limped to the ambulance, since I couldn't lift my leg to climb in the back, the police grabbed me on both sides and shoved me in like a sack of potatoes, I fell flat on my face. The doctor, realizing my condition and that it was severe, gave me a shot of methadone. The relief was immediate.[41]

Behavioral Therapies

Professionals recommend that any narcotic addict seeking recovery enroll in a behavioral therapy program. Behavioral therapy offers understanding and emotional support to the addict, while teaching new techniques for coping with life without narcotics. There are many kinds of behavioral therapy. Some are available from professional counselors and medical practitioners. Professional programs can be operated on either an inpatient or outpatient basis. In an outpatient program, the patient attends a clinic

Homeless addicts can receive help via treatment programs. Many cities have comprehensive residential programs designed specifically for the homeless.

or program in the daytime, then goes home every night. Such programs work well for people with jobs or children. Many of these are supported by hospitals, communities, and local governments. In residential or inpatient programs, the addict lives at the treatment center for a few weeks or months. Odyssey House, Daytop, and Phoenix House are residential centers where addicts work together to build a new life. Both in- and outpatient programs have proven successful, so addicts choose the one that best fits their needs.

In New York, homeless addicts have access to a comprehensive residential treatment program that includes detoxification, methadone, counseling, emotional support, and continuing education. Kevin Rivers is one of New York's many success stories. Counselors describe the changes in Kevin's life:

Kevin Rivers started down the wrong road early: he shot heroin at the age of 12. Unfortunately, giving it up was not as easy, and Kevin spent the next 32 years either on drugs or in jail.

After being released from Riker's Island [prison] the last time, Kevin went to Bellevue Men's shelter. By now, Kevin was on methadone maintenance to control his heroin addiction. While at Bellevue, he heard a speaker from Project Renewal talk about their new program at Kenton Hall—a modified therapeutic community for homeless men on methadone—the first in the city, and probably the country. But . . . he was still using [heroin].

His case manager . . . never gave up on him and gave him constant support. [Kevin says,] "I don't know, I guess she saw something in me that I didn't see." Kevin had joined the culinary arts program but was coming to class high. He was pulled out of class. His case manager and other counselors convinced him to detox. He completed detox, was let back into culinary arts, but again got caught using. His case manager and counselors took him on . . . again. Kevin couldn't understand why they cared so much about him when he didn't. [He said,] "After that I never picked up again. From there it was an uphill battle."

Kevin became immersed in the culinary arts program. [He explained,] "I just needed something to do." Whenever he felt the urge to get high he picked up his books. He just kept reminding himself of what he had to do. After a while he didn't have to remind himself so much and realized that he liked studying and learning more than he liked worrying about getting high. Other people started to notice the change as well and supported him. This made Kevin feel really good. He started to like himself again. [Kevin said,] "I know I can't change the past and what I have done but I can change the future and my way of thinking." He is now working part time and hopes to be hired full time. [He asserts,] "I am a miracle."[42]

Narcotics Anonymous

Several self-help behavioral therapies are conducted by nonmedical personnel. Narcotic Anonymous (NA) is a community-based program made up of former addicts who assist current addicts in getting off and staying off of drugs. In 1947 in Lexington, Kentucky, the first NA meeting was conducted with federal funds by counselors in the public health service. Today, members of NA work closely with medical professionals and social workers who help individuals take twelve specific steps to reach a drug-free life. The goal is to support addicts on their quest for a new, more satisfying life without drugs. There are more than twenty thousand facilities located in seventy countries.

One user tells his story, which is similar to the experiences of other NA members:

My name is Brian and I'm an addict. I choose not to use drugs today. These two sentences give me the right to belong to NA. In the 12 Traditions of Narcotics Anonymous, it says "The only requirement for membership is the desire to stop using." I have that desire.

I spent 14 years in active addiction, and for almost every day of those 14 years I used drugs. When I first started using, I thought they were the greatest thing on earth. I still remember thinking that first time that I would never need to rely on anyone to make me happy ever again. All I needed was my drugs. I used daily from the start. . . . Within a year, I knew I was in trouble and unable to stop.

I could no longer relate to being straight. Normal for me was to be stoned on drugs. There came a time when I had finally had enough and I realised that I would never stop on my own as I had finally accepted to my very soul that I was powerless over drugs and I needed help.

I went for treatment. . . . I was also introduced to the 12 step programme of Narcotics Anonymous. I was told to go to NA when I left treatment if I wanted to stay clean. So I did. I have stayed clean and sober for nine years now on a daily basis thanks to a loving God and the people in NA.[43]

Help Is Everywhere

On March 11, 2002, ABC news reporter Alexa Pozniak shared the success story of one young heroin addict in "Help Is Out There, Treatment for Young Drug Addicts."

By the age of 18, Melanie was a recovering drug addict who had been using both street and prescription drugs for more than five years.

She said, "Drugs were ruining my life. I lost a lot of friends, my relationship with my parents was ridiculous. Everything seems to crumble and you don't seem to realize it . . . I found out about a clinic from kids on the street."

The treatment program that Melanie sought out . . . is funded by the National Institute on Drug Abuse to develop an effective treatment program for young addicts. . . . The 28-day program is set up so that kids are given a combination of medical detox, which includes medication, and lots of intensive counseling.

Although she had been a drug user for many years, Melanie admits her parents never knew about it. . . .

"I told them the day before I entered treatment and they were totally shocked," she says, adding that her parents were very supportive throughout her treatment. . . .

As Melanie looks back, she wishes she received more education about drugs.

"I can't emphasize enough how much these kids have no idea what they're getting themselves into. If I had known what heroin does to people, I probably wouldn't be sitting here talking to you. Kids need to know that they can go anywhere for help, guidance counselors, teachers, friends. The information and help is out there, everywhere. Even though it's intimidating to go up to someone and ask for help, it's important."

Needle Exchange

One focus of harm reduction programs is to help people stay as healthy as possible. Maintaining good health involves many practices, such as adequate nutrition, basic medical care, and the resources to avoid exposure to diseases. Addicts who inject drugs are at risk of contracting contagious bloodborne diseases. In fact, three-quarters of all new cases of AIDS result from intravenous drug use. Addicts who do not have access to clean needles may inject with needles that other people have used.

To slow the spread of bloodborne diseases, more than one hundred cities in the United States have set up clinics to exchange used needles for clean ones. Addicts can also pick up alcohol swabs and get medical advice on the safest ways to shoot up. The Washington State Department of Social and Health Services presented evidence to support the usefulness of needle exchange clinics, stating that,

> Studies have shown that cities which implemented needle exchange programs early in the AIDS epidemic have much lower infection rates among injection drug users than those who waited to implement them. Needle exchange programs act as gateways to drug treatment and other services. Exchange sites are the leading source of drug treatment referral in Washington State.[44]

Many residents of neighborhoods near the treatment centers are not thrilled with the programs, claiming that the centers attract drug users. Nancy Sausman of New York City's Lower East Side says that the programs are "distribution centers for needles and drug paraphernalia. They have nothing to do with health and only work to bring down communities."[45] James Curtis, director

Two addicts collect syringes for a needle exchange. Many clinics exchange clean needles for used ones to prevent the spread of diseases like AIDS.

of psychiatry and addiction at Harlem Hospital Center in New York City, also opposes the program, stating that "Addicts need to be treated. . . . They should not be given needles and encouraged to continue their addiction."[46]

Safe Injection Sites

An even more controversial harm reduction proposal is the establishment of safe injection sites (SIFs). Some countries, including Australia, Switzerland, Germany, and the Netherlands, already have such programs, and Canada is considering them. At these sites, addicts can bring in their drugs, inject using clean equipment, and receive supervision from medically trained personnel. The drugs are not provided for clients by the SIFs, and the staff cannot administer the drugs. Like needle exchange programs, SIFs provide clean equipment. Personnel at these sites also counsel clients, provide medical care, and help get those who are ready into treatment programs.

Critics of SIFs feel that the centers merely encourage drug use and attract addicts to the area. Advocates of SIFs explain that the medical staff helps reduce overdoses and the spread of contagious diseases. The facilities also get addicts off the street and provide a safe place to dispose of used needles.

The director of a new SIF in Sydney, Australia, says that in the first six months of operation, the facility has already saved the lives of 36 people who had overdosed. With 831 registered to use the site, the medical staff sees about 100 people each day. Of these, they have referred 258 to addiction treatment services, health care facilities, or social services for help.

The Whole Picture

Narcotic addiction is a national health problem, yet no one knows the best way to treat it. The most successful programs are those that combine detoxification with support techniques that fit each person's lifestyle and goals. Both chemical and behavioral therapies play important roles in recovery from narcotic addiction.

The future looks hopeful. Research on drug addiction treatment continues. Scientists have already discovered the genetic information that creates opiate receptors on cells. They plan to use this knowledge to make copies, or clones, of receptors in the lab where they can be closely studied. With a better understanding of how receptors work, scientists will be one step closer to understanding the mechanisms of narcotic addiction and discovering more successful treatments.

Chapter 5

Battles in the Drug War

The war against illegal drugs is ongoing. For more than a century, America has taken up the banner opposing the use of drugs that are considered dangerous. Joined by like-minded citizens of other nations, Americans are working on multiple fronts to address the problems that drive people to use illegal drugs, help those who are already victim to them, and above all, eliminate drug sources.

The use of opiates and other illegal drugs became problematic during the late 1800s when opium dens emerged. By 1900 the popularity of opium dens had spread through the entire country. Many cities attempted to eradicate them by creating local ordinances that banned opium smoking.

On a national level, few laws protected citizens from dangerous drugs. One of the first was the Pure Food and Drug Act which was passed by Congress in 1906. This law required that the medicine industry post the ingredients of their formulations on the bottles so that consumers would know what they were buying. The Pure Food and Drug Act was necessary because most citizens had no idea that commonly used elixirs and remedies contained opium, morphine, and heroin.

However, at that time the U.S. government had never outlawed the sale or use of any drugs. The federal government, which believed in state control of issues, was reluctant to step forward and take charge of the growing drug problem. States were left on their own to handle drug issues. Several had placed restrictions on drug use, but these varied from state to state. Many contended that laws passed at the state level were not solving growing drug problems.

Reformers pressed the need for such laws, arguing that the national government was better equipped to handle drug problems than the individual states. Also, they felt that, as a nation, the United States needed to take a formal position against the nonmedical use of narcotics. In response, Congress passed the Smoking Opium Exclusion Act in 1909 which prohibited the importation of opium that had been processed or prepared for smoking.

Users are depicted in a Chinese opium den. Because the drug was regularly used for nonmedical purposes, opium use was banned by Congress in 1909.

It was not local reformers who finally goaded the government into making more comprehensive national drug laws. Rather, progress against the use of narcotics on the international level forced the United States to act. In 1910 the United States and other countries helped China close the opium industry in that country. One year later, forty-six countries attended the First International Conference on Opium at the Hague. Most diplomats, including those from the United States, agreed to discourage the use of narcotics in their own countries. In a document called the Opium Convention, each nation promised to control narcotics in its own country through domestic laws. As a key player in the conference, the United States felt that it must hold up its end of the bargain.

The Federal Government Steps Forward

In 1914 the federal government took a critical step toward limiting the use of narcotics by passing the Harrison Narcotics Act. This act stated that only doctors and pharmacists could buy, sell, or dispense opiates, and those who did must first register with the federal government, then pay a tax to the Internal Revenue Service. Additionally all transactions relating to heroin had to be recorded. The punishment for not doing so was a fine and a prison sentence. The need for a tax-collecting agency to assess penalties on those who disobeyed this new law led to the development of the Bureau of Narcotics.

The Harrison Narcotics Act had a tremendous impact on two groups of people, the addicts and the medical community who had been working with them. The addicts were in a bad position for several reasons. Once the Harrison Act went into effect, it became very difficult to get opiates. At the same time, the status of addicts fell in the public's opinion; they were no longer viewed as victims of faulty medical treatment but as social outcasts. One young heroin user, Leroy Street of New York, said that because of the act, he was now "one of a band set apart by the will of society, too, and harried for our nonconformity. At least it seemed to me that we were being persecuted only because we were different, not because we were dangerous."[47]

Taking the Cure

In his 1998 history of drugs in America, *Drug Crazy*, Mike Gray explained that when Congress passed the Harrison Narcotics Act in 1914, it did not intend to make the lives of narcotic users more difficult. Most congressmen believed that they were helping the addicts, who could be easily cured. Part of their misperception arose from the release in 1909 of a so-called miracle cure that was supposed to end any type of drug addiction within just a few days.

The perpetuator of this medical hoax was not a doctor, but a former insurance salesman from Georgia named Charles Towns. His secret formula was a strong laxative. To test its effectiveness, Towns kidnapped a homeless heroin addict and locked him in a hotel room. After the first dose of gut-wrenching "cure," the unwilling subject tried to commit suicide. Forty-eight hours into the "treatment," the addict was offered a syringe of his drug. To Towns's delight, he declined it and Towns rewarded him with his freedom.

Armed with his wonder product, Towns went to the country's leading researchers in drug abuse and addiction. One of these, Alexander Lambert of Cornell University, agreed to let Towns demonstrate his product on some hospitalized addicts. After just one week of treatment, addicts left the hospital claiming to be new men. None returned for their follow-up treatments—apparently because they were cured.

Lambert, also the personal physician of President Theodore Roosevelt, was impressed with the results. In short order, the doctor told everyone in Washington about the miracle cure. Lawmakers were so delighted to have a cure available that no one asked questions about its reliability.

Ten years later, Lambert checked on some of Towns's former patients. Fully 95 percent of the patients who had sought treatment at the hospital had returned to drug use. Lambert's investigation revealed that the drug cure and Towns were frauds. However, by then, the U.S. government had adopted an unforgiving attitude toward addicts that persisted for decades.

Addicts looked for treatment programs, but there were very few available. Thousands of addicts who turned to the medical community found an unexpected cold shoulder there. Large numbers of doctors decided to avoid them because the Harrison Act made it cumbersome and complicated to treat them.

The few doctors willing to treat addicts found themselves in an awkward situation. Under the Harrison Act, doctors and pharmacists assumed that they could care for drug addicts in the way they saw fit as long as they completed all the required paperwork. Therefore, many of those who treated addicts continued writing prescriptions for maintenance doses of opiates. But the Treasury Department frowned on this practice because it wanted to end the use of drugs. Consequently, it required that doctors write prescriptions for increasingly smaller doses with the goal of weaning addicts off their drugs. The logic was based on a long-held, but erroneous, belief that addiction could be easily cured under a doctor's care. No one realized that even if a doctor could help a patient stop using drugs, the rate of relapse was extremely high.

Many doctors and druggists who found it impossible to wean addicts off of their drug habits continued to write prescriptions for maintenance doses. As a result, they were arrested and fined.

Many doctors in the early twentieth century wrote prescriptions for opiates because they were unable to treat addiction.

John Hoffman, a historian, describes the doctors' plight.

> The Act was intended to prohibit recreational use of opiates and to only al-
> low doctors to prescribe them in "good faith" as part of a legitimate med-
> ical practice. Although the term "good faith" may have originally been
> ambiguous, the zealous nature of U.S. Treasury agents . . . soon made this
> term quite clear. The overall effect of the Harrison Act was to prohibit most
> medical use of opiates. Treasury agents responsible for enforcement of the
> Act were quick to investigate and to prosecute opiate-prescribing physi-
> cians. In fact, between 1915 and 1938, over 25,000 doctors were reported
> to the authorities for violating the Harrison Act. It is not surprising that the
> medical community began to shun the use of the opiates not only for treat-
> ing the addicted but also for treating the organically ill.[48]

A New Market Niche

Once drugs were outlawed, addicts who bought them had to do
so on the illegal black market. The scarcity of morphine and
heroin caused the prices to skyrocket. The cost of an ounce of
heroin rose dramatically from $6.50 to about $100. Many addicts
found themselves without enough money to buy drugs at their
newly inflated prices. As a result, they turned to crime to secure
the funds they needed.

New York City saw a rapid increase in crime following the pas-
sage of the Harrison Act and tried to combat the problem by
opening the Worth Street Clinic in 1919. There, addicts received
the drugs they craved and used them under medical supervision.
In the early months, about 1,000 addicts a day filed through.
Eventually, the clinic began to push the Treasury Department's
goal to wean addicts off drugs. Each week, the clinicians handed
out smaller and smaller doses. Many addicts were not interested in
the government's ideas to reduce their drug consumption, so
when government reduced its doses, they bought supplements of
narcotics on the street. Only 2,000 of the clients agreed to enroll
in the drug recovery program at the clinic. Of those, 150 stayed
with the program. The program offered at Worth Street Clinic
was so ineffective that even the few people who were able to stop
using drugs under medical treatment suffered a 90 percent relapse

Arnold Rothstein, a crime boss in the 1920s, boosted the drug trade in America by smuggling narcotics from Europe.

rate. Fifty other cities opened similar clinics, but none were very successful in helping addicts give up their drugs.

The Harrison Act unintentionally provided a lucrative business opportunity for others. With so few places for addicts to buy drugs, a new market appeared; a market of thousands who desperately wanted to purchase heroin. Arnold Rothstein was one of the many crime bosses who took advantage of this market in the 1920s.

Rothstein, an innovator of sorts, created a system of smuggling illegal drugs into the United States. Rothstein knew that drug pushers in the New York area had very little stock to sell. What they did have was either smuggled in from China, stolen from drug-manufacturing companies, or ordered from manufacturers by fake companies that set up temporary addresses in Mexico.

None of these sources could supply the large amounts of opiates that Rothstein needed for the market.

Rothstein sent his representatives to legitimate drug manufacturers in Europe. There, they bought hundreds of pounds of narcotics with no questions asked by the sellers. These purchases were crated, labeled as plumbing supplies, engine parts, or some other bogus item, then shipped to the United States. Rothstein's stateside men picked up the shipments at the ports and distributed their contents to sellers in the major cities. In no time, other criminals were copying Rothstein's techniques and illegal drugs poured into America's harbors. However, by 1930, authorities had figured out Rothstein's ruse and seized the drugs as fast as they arrived on American soil. As a result, many illegal drug entrepreneurs went out of business.

By the time World War II began, illegal drugs became scarce again. Most illegal sources, like Rothstein's operation, had been closed down, and the war front required all the legal pharmaceuticals that could be manufactured. For a short time, it seemed as if the epidemic of drug use had ended. By the end of the war, public health officials estimated that the number of addicts was only one in every three thousand people, down by tenfold since 1900. This slowing of narcotic sales marked the end of a period that some call America's First Drug Epidemic.

The Second Attack, 1950–1970

Throughout the 1950s and 1960s the number of heroin users rose once again. Most of the heroin sold in the United States was smuggled in from Asia. One region in particular, the Golden Triangle, had a long history as a source of opium. In the highlands of Southeast Asia, sections of Burma, Thailand, and Laos, opium is still grown in remote areas by poor farmers. These Asian farmers sold their raw opium to middlemen in Marseille, France, a group known as the "French Connection." French buyers processed the crude product into heroin. Sicilian and Corsican Mafias, criminal organizations who had dealt in drugs before, delivered the finished products to crime bosses in the United States.

Throughout the 1960s and 1970s, the Mafias ran extensive networks to distribute their illegal goods. As the numbers of users swelled through the 1970s, government officials worried that the American way of life might be in danger. By the time Nixon came into office, drug use was up in the United States, with estimates of 750,000 heroin addicts. Nixon was concerned about drug use by soldiers in Vietnam and demanded that they be tested. For the first time, the army found out that it had a sizable drug problem. Fearing that heroin abuse would compromise U.S. effectiveness in Vietnam, and alarmed by the growing number of addicts at home, Nixon launched a full-fledged war on drugs and First Lady Patricia Nixon led a "Just Say No" campaign that targeted children.

American soldiers in Vietnam exchange vials of heroin. The problem of narcotics in the military first came to light when soldiers underwent drug tests.

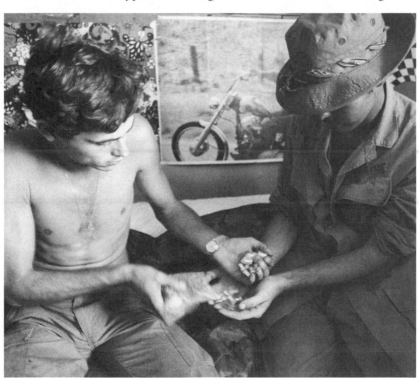

Making a Drug Illegal

One front of the drug war centered on reducing the availability of dangerous drugs. In 1970 Congress passed the Comprehensive Drug Abuse and Prevention Act in an effort to control the use of drugs by U.S. citizens. Title II of the act, a section referred to as the Controlled Substances Act (CSA), laid out the guidelines for restricting the use of drugs. Congress did not use the chemical characteristics of drugs as a measure of their menace. Instead, they classified the drugs that were most likely to be abused as the most dangerous. Schedule I drugs are those with the greatest potential for abuse and no approved medical use. From a legal point of

---

Nixon Promises Help for Vietnam Vets

The availability of heroin in Vietnam caused unexpected problems for U.S. forces and eventually led Nixon to declare a war on drugs. Many servicemen tried heroin, an attractive deterrent to concerns about combat, for the first time. Recorded in *The Consumer's Union Report on Licit and Illicit Drugs* by Edward M. Brecher and the editors of *Consumer Reports* magazine, 1972, one soldier explained how he was introduced to heroin. "I had my all-expense-paid vacation in sunny SE Asia in 1970–71. I still remember stepping off base onto Highway 1 at Phu Bai Combat Base south of Hue one mid-morning and being approached by a kid about ten years old who had jumped off the back of a cyclo to offer me a small vial of heroin ('skag') for only two dollars."

During 1971, the media reported that addiction among soldiers ran as high as 10 to 15 percent, a figure that many found unbelievable. However, among 930 returnees passing through the Oakland, California, army terminal who voluntarily filled out anonymous questions, 16 percent confirmed that they had indeed used heroin within the last thirty days.

News coverage of the heroin "epidemic" among servicemen spurred the White House into action. In 1971 President Richard Nixon's message to Congress called for extra funding to help soldiers returning from Vietnam beat their narcotic addiction. Nixon's request for financial help, recorded in *The Consumer's Union Report on Licit and Illicit Drugs*, struck the hearts of Americans: "The Department of Defense will provide rehabilitation programs to all servicemen being returned for discharge who want this help, and we will be requesting legislation to permit the military services to retain for treatment any individual due for discharge who is a narcotic addict."

view, abuse refers to use of a drug or other substance in a manner that is not approved by the government. Heroin is a Schedule I drug. Schedule II includes all the drugs with a high potential for abuse that have a medical use. Morphine, codeine, and most of the synthetic opiates fall in this category.

Strategies to Win the Drug War

The drug war had many fronts; another focus was on eliminating drug sources at an international level. The United States helped the Turkish government make all poppy growing illegal. At the same time, it supported the French government's efforts to eliminate the Corsican syndicate's heroin lab in Paris. Within a few years, some short-term successes were obvious. By the end of the Vietnam War, the amount of heroin flowing into America had slowed.

However, like any article of trade, loss in one area spurred growth in another. Without the Asian connection, buyers sought new markets and quickly turned to sources in Mexico, South America, and the Golden Crescent, an area that includes sections of Iran, Afghanistan, and Pakistan.

With each change in White House administration, the U.S. drug war strategy fluctuated. Source elimination aimed to stop the flow of drugs into this country by eliminating their sources in other countries. To replace the income of impoverished opium growers, the United States helped teach farmers how to raise other crops that had high market value. Interdiction focused on stopping smugglers who carried drugs into the United States. Education centered on teaching young people the dangers of drug use.

Worldwide Attack

In a special meeting of the General Assembly of the United Nations in 1998, representatives emphasized the need to not just reduce the global supply of drugs, but also the demand. In a document called the Political Declaration on the Guiding Principles of Drug Demand Reduction, member countries of the United Nations made commitments to lower the supply as well as

The United Nations addressed the global drug issue in 1998. Participating countries work to diminish narcotics use and improve drug awareness.

the demand for drugs by 2008. The United Nations Commission on Narcotic Drugs supports several programs, all of which are aimed at reducing illegal narcotic use and sales.

The commission provides assistance to participating countries in many ways. It recommends the implementation of programs that support people whose lives are jeopardized by narcotic use. It also endorses the establishment of more drug treatment facilities and is active in plans to slow the spread of HIV by intravenous drug users.

Progress is difficult to assess because each signing nation chooses its own methods for reducing supplies of narcotics and for educating and treating its citizens. However, some strides are clear. The greatest achievement of the commission may be its success in getting countries to help one another do away with opium crops. Currently, it is working closely with central Asian countries to wipe out sources of opiates there. It also concentrates much of its energy on assisting the Afghan government in eliminating narcotics in that country. This help is especially valuable in a time when opium crops have been plentiful and sales for illicit growers are promising. According to the commission's executive director, Antonio Maria Costa, "the annual Afghanistan Opium Survey for 2002, conducted by the United Nations Office on Drugs and Crime, has confirmed earlier indications of the considerable level of opium production in the country this year."[49] He called for greater international assistance in helping Afghanistan eliminate opium, a step that will also help the rest of the world reduce opium availability.

The Challenges

While both the United Nations and the United States assist the Afghan government's efforts to eliminate opium, the eyes of the

The Opium Crop

In the July 2001 *Worcester Telegram & Gazette*, Emilie Astell helps the reader understand some of the complex issues involved in eliminating opium farms.

Astell profiles Robert Bouvier, a member of the UN International Drug Control Program. He is visiting the farmers who live in a region now known as Myanmar, formerly Burma, to assess the impact of opium on individual lives, the community, the ecology, and the economy. When he has completed this assessment, he hopes to make some recommendations to help the local farmers find a new strategy for earning money.

About twenty-five thousand people live in the Wa zone of Myanmar. Many of them grow poppies on their small farms, producing about seven pounds of opium per half acre. Each pound can be sold for about $40, providing the families with a mere $140 each year. Many families prefer to trade their opium than to sell it, swapping their year's crop for fourteen hundred pounds of rice. Opium farmers save a portion of their opium for personal use, primarily to treat painful conditions like toothache, because most cannot afford to spend several days traveling to a health care facility.

Bouvier knows that governmental changes are on the way. Authorities may ban opium farming in Myanmar. Without their income from opium, some will have to cut down the trees around the villages so they can plant large fields of less profitable crops. Many families who are just getting by may be pushed to the brink of starvation. Despite his concerns and efforts to quickly help these farmers find a better way to earn a living, Bouvier knows that finding a solution to this complex problem may take a while.

world track their progress. In a country where poverty and war-lords control life, getting rid of opium is a challenge. Reporter Maureen Orth reveals how poverty drives some people to raise opium poppies and sell their products, despite huge personal risks:

> The entire population is engaged in smuggling the only cash crop that Afghanistan grows, the opium poppy. You have to smuggle or die of star-vation—it is the only means to live. There is nothing else for them (the lo-cal people) economically. Even in the middle of winter, villagers . . . jump barefoot into the icy water to float kilos of heroin across the river inside animals skins tacked on old inner tubes or rubber rafts. . . . A billion-dollar industry depends on a guy pushing an animal skin across a freezing river.[50]

However, the destruction of the Afghan opium business is well underway. In Colombia, UN officials know that loss of opium supplies in one part of the world will only drive up sales in an-other, so they wait for the backlash. Even though Colombian opium farms are small in comparison to the Asian suppliers, Colombian growers will try to fill the market niche created by the loss of Afghan products. An international drug-control official ex-

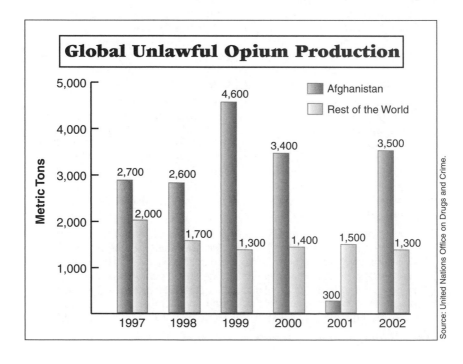

Source: United Nations Office on Drugs and Crime.

plains his prediction simply: "So it makes sense that there should be more opium poppy grown in Colombia than before."[51]

As in any business, demand drives the market. As long as the world's addicts desire narcotics, someone will supply opium products to them.

Narcotics: For Better or Worse

Clearly, global disapproval of illegal drugs is growing. Under the leadership of the United Nations, countries work closely together to reduce supplies of drugs all over the world. Yet, even in the United States, opinions about progress and success in the drug war range widely. Critics point out that, despite decades of governmental laws and restrictions, narcotic use in this country persists and that the war on drugs is a total failure.

David Boaz, reporting in the *Freedom Daily*, expresses the frustration felt by many over this "war": "More than $30 billion is being spent annually on the drug war. One and a half million people are being arrested every year. But 78 million people say they have tried drugs, and 80 percent of teenagers say drugs are easy to obtain. Things are obviously going in the wrong direction."[52]

Supporters of the drug war praise the government's efforts to protect Americans from drugs. Many feel that campaigns to prevent drug use have influenced a large number of people to decide against using drugs. Asa Hutchinson, director of the Drug Enforcement Administration, said in June 2002, "Overall drug use in the United States is down 50%; since the late 1970s. . . . And we've reduced the number of *chronic* heroin users over the last decades."[53] Others suggest that government efforts have significantly reduced the consequences of drug use in society such as crime and poverty among users.

Clearly, no one knows the best solution, but several organizations are determined to find it. The United Nations, currently working with 168 countries, is expanding its strategies to both slow the production of opiates and reduce the number of people who want them. Perhaps the answers to the world's drug problem will soon be within grasp.

Notes

Introduction: The Many Faces of Narcotics

1. Mike Gray, *Drug Crazy*. New York: Random House, 1998, p. 52.

Chapter 1: Narcotics, the "Milk of Paradise"

2. Quoted in Dean Latimer and Jeff Goldberg, *Flowers in the Blood: The Story of Opium*. New York: Franklin Watts, 1981, pp. 6–7.
3. Quoted in Latimer and Goldberg, *Flowers in the Blood*, p. 19.
4. Quoted in *A Brief History of Opium*, 1999. http://opiates.net.
5. Quoted in Latimer and Goldberg, *Flowers in the Blood*, p. 47.
6. Quoted in "The Plant of Joy."
7. Quoted in "The Plant of Joy."
8. Thomas De Quincey, "Confessions of an English Opium-Eater," *London Magazine*, 1821. http://opioids.com.
9. Quoted in Latimer and Goldberg, *Flowers in the Blood*, pp. 85–86.
10. Quoted in "The Plant of Joy."
11. Quoted in John Wilcock, "Guilty Gardeners?" Chris Ridder's Home Page. www.cridder.com.
12. Quoted in Wilcock, "Guilty Gardeners?"
13. Quoted in Wilcock, "Guilty Gardeners?"
14. Solomon H. Snyder, *Drugs and the Brain*. New York: Scientific American Library, 1986, p. 44.
15. Snyder, *Drugs and the Brain*, p. 44.
16. Snyder, *Drugs and the Brain*, p. 47.

Chapter 2: Search for the Perfect Painkiller

17. Quoted in William White, Earnest Kurtz, and Caroline Acker, "The Combined Addiction Disease Chronologies, 5th

BC to 1863," *Behavioral Health Recovery Management*. www.bhrm.org.

18. Martin Booth, *Opium, a History*. New York: St. Martin's, 1996, p. 73.

19. Quoted in Edward M. Brecher, "Opiates for Relief, for Tranquilization, and Pleasure," *Consumer's Union Report on Licit and Illicit Drugs, Schaffer Library*, 1972. www.druglibrary.org.

20. Quoted in Jill Jones, *Hep Cats, Narcs, and Pipe Dreams*. New York: Scribner, 1996, p.19.

21. John Witherspoon, "Oration on Medicine: A Protest Against Some of the Evils in the Profession of Medicine," *Journal of the American Medical Association*, 1900. www.druglibrary.org.

22. Quoted in *United Nations Bulletin on Narcotics*, April–June 1953, "Heroin: The History of a 'Miracle Drug.'" www.drugtext.org.

23. Quoted in Richard Askwith, "How Aspirin Turned Hero," *Sunday Times*, September 13, 1998. www.opioids.com.

24. John D. Trawick, "A Case of Heroin Poisoning," *Kentucky Medical Journal*, vol. 9, no. 187, *United Nations Office on Drugs and Crime*, 1953. www.undcp.org.

25. Quoted in *Narconon of Northern California*, "An Addict's Story." www.heroinabuse.net.

26. Trout, "Heroin & Ecstasy," *Erowid Experience Vault*, June 27, 2001. www.erowid.org.

27. Travis, "Nothingness," *Erowid Experience Vault*, October 18, 2000. www.erowid.org.

Chapter 3: Narcotic Addiction and Abuse

28. Quoted in Charity McIver, "'I Was a Heroin Addict,' Story of a Maryland Youth, a Personal Account," *ABCnews.com*, August 22, 2001. http://abcnews.go.com.

29. Quoted in *Teen Challenge*, Drug Information Section, "Physical Signs of Heroin Usage," 2000. www.teenchallenge.com.

30. Quoted in Andrew Weil and Winifred Rosen, *From Chocolate to Morphine*. New York: Houghton Mifflin, 1993, p. 89.

31. GizmoMan, "The Reverse Progression," *alt.drugs.hard*, September 18, 1996. http://balder.prohosting.com.

32. Quoted in Rob Goodspeed, "Autopsy: Death Caused by Heroin Use," *Michigan Daily Online*, April 8, 2002. www.michigandaily.com.

33. Quoted in William Tinker, "Heroin Use Up in Ma.," *Worcester Telegram and Gazette*, December 10, 2001. http://projects. is.asu.edu.

34. Will, "My Friend Harry," *Erowid Experience Vaults*, September 11, 2000. www.erowid.org.

35. Quoted in Polly Saltonstall, "Born Addicted," *Standard-Times*, May 30, 1999. www.s-t.com.

Chapter 4: Treatment of Narcotic Addiction

36. Zeina, "Heroin Pages Past Letter Page," *Heroin Pages*, January 2002. www.heroinpages.org.

37. Quoted in Paul M. Gahlinger, *Illegal Drugs*. Sagebrush, 2001, p. 379.

38. David Costello, "Clean and Sober in 48 Hours?" *Los Angeles Times*, October 28, 2002. www.methodone-detox.com.

39. Chris, "Heroin Pages Past Letter Page," *Heroin Pages*, January 2002. www.heroinpages.org.

40. Weil and Rosen, *From Chocolate to Morphine*, p. 89.

41. Quoted in *Narconon*, "Methadone and Methadone Addiction." www.heroinaddiction.com.

42. Quoted in *Project Renewal*, "Addiction." www.projectrenewal. org.

43. *Brian's Recovery Page*, "My Story." http://homepages.ihug. co.nz.

44. Washington State Department of Social and Health Services, Division of Alcohol and Substance Abuse, "Policy Issues Confronting Washington State, Needle Exchange Programs," February 9, 2002. www.2.dshs.wa.gov.

45. Quoted in Janet Firshein, "The Debate over Needle Exchange," *Close to Home Online*. www.pbs.org.

46. Quoted in Craig Horowitz, "Drugs are Bad; the Drug War Is Worse," *New York Magazine*, pp. 22–23, February 5, 1996. www.pdxnormal.org.

Chapter 5: Battles in the Drug War

47. Quoted in Jones, *Hep Cats, Narcs, and Pipe Dreams*, p. 110.
48. John Hoffman, "The Historical Shift in the Perception of Opiates: From Medicine to Social Menace," *CNS*. http://addictionology.com.
49. Quoted in United Nations Information Service, "United Nations Calls for Greater Assistance to Afghans in Fight Against Opium Cultivation," October 24, 2002. www.undcp.org.
50. Maureen Orth, "Afghanistan's Deadly Habit," *Online Edition of Daily News*, January 2, 2003. http://origin.dailynews.lk.
51. Quoted in Kirk Semple, "Colombia: Afghan Effort May Shift Heroin Sales," *Boston Globe*, January 20, 2002. www.mapinc.org.
52. David Boaz, "Time to Rethink the War on Drugs," Future of Freedom Foundation, October 1999. www.fff.org.
53. Asa Hutchinson, "Modernizing Criminal Justice," *Drug Enforcement Administration Home*, June 18, 2002. www.usdoj.gov.

Organizations to Contact

Narconon Northern California
262 Gaffey Rd.
Watsonville, CA 95076
(831) 768-7190
www.drugrehab.net

Narconon has sites all over the United States that are dedicated to helping addicts without chemical intervention.

Narcotics Anonymous
PO Box 999
Van Nuys, CA 91409
(818) 780-3951
www.na.org

Narcotics Anonymous provides peer support to help addicts end their addiction and lead clean, productive lives.

National Institute on Drug Abuse (NIDA)
6001 Executive Blvd., Room 5213
Bethesda, MD 20892-9651
(301) 729-6686
www.drugabuse.gov

The NIDA provides information on research into drug abuse, its causes, and its treatments.

For Further Reading

Books

Bruno Leone, *Chemical Dependency*. San Diego: Greenhaven Press, 1997. A collection of articles on opposing points of view about drug use and treatment of drug addiction.

Geraldine Woods, *Heroin*. Springfield, NJ: Enslow, 1994. An overview of the history and current use of heroin, this book is easy to read and includes interesting personal accounts by addicts.

Websites

Fact Monster (www.factmonster.com). Use the Fact Monster search program to get information on all aspects of narcotic use.

In the Know Zone—Heroin (www.intheknowzone.com). Provides the history of heroin use and abuse in the United States.

Neuroscience for Kids (http://faculty.washington.edu). The site provides a concise and easy-to-read history of heroin use and abuse as well as information on current abuse trends.

Works Consulted

Books

Martin Booth, *Opium, a History*. New York: St. Martin's, 1996. A detailed history of opium, its chemistry, use, and politics.

Carol Falkowski, *Dangerous Drugs*. Center City, MN: Hazelden, 2000. Falkowski provides the reader with an overview of the way drugs are abused and the extent of their use, as well as explanations of their effects on the body, methods of treatment, and suggestions for prevention.

Paul M. Gahlinger, *Illegal Drugs*. Sagebrush, 2001. A comprehensive review of illegal drugs, drug policy, addiction, and treatment.

Mike Gray, *Drug Crazy*. New York: Random House, 1998. A history of opium and cocaine use and abuse in the United States.

Elizabeth Connell Henderson, *Understanding Addiction*. Jackson: University Press of Mississippi, 2000. Designed for the friends and families of addicts, this book explains all aspects of addiction in nonmedical terms.

Jill Jones, *Hep Cats, Narcs, and Pipe Dreams*. New York: Scribner, 1996. Through a collection of essays, Jones describes the history of narcotics use and abuse in the United States.

Dean Latimer and Jeff Goldberg, *Flowers in the Blood: The Story of Opium*. New York: Franklin Watts, 1981. A fun-to-read history of narcotics.

Solomon H. Snyder, *Drugs and the Brain*. New York: Scientific American Library, 1986. Recounts early research on how narcotics affect the brain, including the discovery of opiate receptors.

Joseph Sora, *The Reference Shelf, Substance Abuse.* New York: H.W. Wilson, 1997. Reprints from books, articles, and addresses on trends in drug use in the United States.

Andrew Weil and Winifred Rosen, *From Chocolate to Morphine.* New York: Houghton Mifflin, 1993. Provides information about mind-altering drugs in straightforward language.

Mark Yoslow, *Drugs in the Body.* New York: Franklin Watts, 1992. A comprehensive look at the physiological effects of several drugs on body chemistry.

Internet Sources

Serena Altschul, "Addicted: An OxyContin Tragedy," *48 Hours Investigates,* August 23, 2002. www.cbsnews.com.

American RSD Hope Group, "The Quality of Mercy," 2000. www.rsdhope.org.

Richard Askwith, "How Aspirin Turned Hero," *Sunday Times,* September 13, 1998. www.opioids.com.

Associated Press, "Son's Oxycontin Overdose Death Sets Father on Crusade Against Drug Dealers," August 25, 2002. www.intelihealth.com.

Emilie Astell, "Couple Working to Weaken Opium's Grip," *Worcester Telegram & Gazette,* July 9, 2001. www.poppy.org.

David Boaz, "Time to Rethink the War on Drugs," Future of Freedom Foundation, October 1999. www.fff.org.

Edward M. Brecher, "Opiates for Relief, for Tranquilization, and Pleasure," *Consumer's Union Report on Licit and Illicit Drugs, Schaffer Library,* 1972. www.druglibrary.org.

Brian's Recovery Page, "My Story." http://homepages.ihug.co.nz.

Ralph Carlson, "Rifles, Dope, and Camera," Institute for Advanced Technology in the Humanities, November 27, 1997. http://lists.village.virginia.edu.

Chris, "Heroin Pages Past Letter Page," *Heroin Pages,* January 2002. www.heroinpages.org.

Concerning Heroin, "Inside Philadelphia Heroin Culture," November 12, 2002. www.spies.com.

David Costello, "Clean and Sober in 48 Hours?" *Los Angeles Times*, October 28, 2002. www.methadone-detox.com.

Thomas De Quincey, "Confessions of an English Opium-Eater," *London Magazine*, 1821. http://opioids.com.

Janet Firshein, "The Debate over Needle Exchange," *Close to Home Online*. www.pbs.org.

GizmoMan, "The Reverse Progression," *alt.drugs.hard*, September 18, 1996. http://balder.prohosting.com.

Rob Goodspeed, "Autopsy: Death Caused by Heroin Use," *Michigan Daily Online*, April 8, 2002. www.michigandaily.com.

John Hoffman, "The Historical Shift in the Perception of Opiates: From Medicine to Social Menace," *CNS*. http://addictionology.com.

Craig Horowitz, "Drugs are Bad; the Drug War Is Worse," *New York Magazine*, February 5, 1996. www.pdxnormal.org.

Asa Hutchinson, "Modernizing Criminal Justice," Drug Enforcement Administration Home, June 18, 2002. www.usdoj.gov.

Alan I. Leshner, "Oops: How Casual Drug Use Leads to Addiction," National Institute on Drug Abuse, January 25, 2001. www.nida.nih.gov.

Charity McIver, "'I Was a Heroin Addict,' Story of a Maryland Youth, a Personal Account," *ABCnews.com*, August 22, 2001. http://abcnews.go.com.

Narconon, "Methadone and Methadone Addiction." www.heroinaddiction.com.

Narcanon of Northern California, "An Addict's Story." www.heroinabuse.net.

Maureen Orth, "Afghanistan's Deadly Habit," *Online Edition of Daily News*, January 2, 2003. http://origin.dailynews.lk.

John Patten, "Story of a Heroin User," *Packet Online*, April 8, 2000. www.pacpubserver.com.

Project Renewal, "Addiction." www.projectrenewal.org.

Polly Saltonstall, "Born Addicted," *Standard-Times*, May 30, 1999. www.s-t.com.

Kirk Semple, "Colombia: Afghan Effort May Shift Heroin Sales," *Boston Globe*, January 20, 2002. www.mapinc.org.

Substance Abuse & Mental Health Services Administration, "2001 National Household Survey on Drug Abuse, National Summary of Findings." www.samhsa.gov.

Teen Challenge, Drug Information Section, "Physical Signs of Heroin Usage," 2000. www.teenchallenge.com.

William Tinker, "Heroin Use Up in Ma.," *Worcester Telegram and Gazette*, December 10, 2001. http://projects.is.asu.edu.

Travis, "Nothingness," *Erowid Experience Vault*, October 18, 2000. www.erowid.org.

John D. Trawick, "A Case of Heroin Poisoning," *Kentucky Medical Journal*, vol. 9, no. 187, *United Nations Office on Drugs and Crime*, 1953. www.undcp.org.

Trout, "Heroin & Ecstasy," *Erowid Experience Vault*, June 27, 2001. www.erowid.org.

United Nations Bulletin on Narcotics, April–June 1953, "Heroin: The History of a 'Miracle Drug'." www.drugtext.org.

United Nations Information Service, "United Nations Calls for Greater Assistance to Afghans in Fight Against Opium Cultivation," October 24, 2002. www.undcp.org.

Washington State Department of Social and Health Services, Division of Alcohol and Substance Abuse, "Policy Issues Confronting Washington State, Needle Exchange Programs," February 9, 2002. www.2.dshs.wa.gov.

William White, Earnest Kurtz, and Caroline Acker, "The Combined Addiction Disease Chronologies, 5th BC to 1863," *Behavioral Health Recovery Management*. www.bhrm.org.

John Wilcock, "Guilty Gardeners?" Chris Ridder's Home Page. www.cridder.com.

Will, "My Friend Harry," *Erowid Experience Vaults*, September 11, 2000. www.erowid.org.

John Witherspoon, "Oration on Medicine: A Protest Against Some of the Evils in the Profession of Medicine," *Journal of the American Medical Association*, 1900, www.druglibrary.org.

Zeina, "Heroin Pages Past Letter Page," *Heroin Pages*, January 2002. www.heroinpages.org.

Websites

BBC News (http://news.bbc.co.uk). This website provides news coverage on a variety of issues related to narcotics.

A Brief History of Opium (http://opiates.net). A compilation of quotes from famous narcotic addicts, including Samuel Taylor Coleridge and Thomas De Quincey.

Chinese in Early Deadwood (www.DeadwoodUnderGround.org). Provides history of opium dens in Deadwood, South Dakota.

DEA (www.dea.gov). Excellent source of information about patterns of drug use in the United States. Also carries news stories relating to drug seizures.

Do It Now Foundation (www.doitnow.org). Gives general information about illicit drugs and suggests ways for parents to drug-proof their families.

The Early History of the Poppy and Opium (www.poppies.org). First printed in the *Journal of the Archeological Society of Athens*, this article describes the use of opium in the eastern Mediterranean area.

Heroin Abuse.Net (www.heroinabuse.net). Supported by Narcocon, this website posts diaries and stories written by drug addicts.

Heroin Addiction (www.heroinaddiction.com). This site contains information on all aspects of heroin addiction and treatment, including methadone treatment.

Heroin Pages (www.heroinpages.org). A website where people whose lives have been impacted by heroin share stories and give advice.

Kinsley Police Department, Kinsley, Kansas (www.midway.net). Discusses current law enforcement issues related to illicit use of narcotics.

Los Angeles Weekly, Points of Contention (www.laweekly.com). Provides articles on drug treatment problems in the area, including one on Hollywood's clean-needle exchange program.

Narconon Southern California Opiate Treatment (www.stopopiateabuse.com). Covers all aspects of opiate use, including historical and political perspectives.

Narcotic (www.addictions.org). Provides general information about narcotics.

Narcotics Anonymous (www.na.org). A website that explains the mission, purpose, and rules of membership in Narcotics Anonymous.

National Institute of Drug Abuse (www.drugabuse.gov). Contains research on narcotic abuse and addiction.

New York Magazine (www.pdxnormal.org). Carries story by Craig Horowitz that explains why the war on drugs is not making any progress.

Opioids: Past, Present, and Future (http://opioids.com). Excerpts from Thomas De Quincey's book *Confessions of an English Opium-Eater.*

PBS, the Debate over Needle Exchange (www.pbs.org). Examines the pros and cons of a clean-needle exchange program.

Poppies.Org (www.poppies.org). Features news articles related to narcotics.

Project Renewal (www.projectrenewal.org). Presents addiction treatment programs in New York City, along with personal success stories.

RWJF Grant Results Report: Additional Analyses in a Study of the Development of Narcotics (www.rwjf.org). Provides findings of research on early predictors of narcotic addiction.

Saginaw Bay Area Narcotic Anonymous Resources (http://michigan-na.org). Provides help on a variety of topics related to narcotic abuse, including stories written by former narcotics abusers.

Schaffer Library (www.druglibrary.org). A site on the history of drug use and drug policy in the United States.

United Nations Drug Control Program (www.undcp.org). This site provides up-to-date information on the activities on the UNDCP.

The Vaults of Erowid (www.erowid.org). A collection of information about illicit drug use, including articles from newspapers, scientific data from research studies, and personal accounts.

Index

Picture Credits

Cover photo: Associated Press, AP
Associated Press, AP, 64, 66
© Annie Griffiths Belt/CORBIS, 74
© Bettmann/CORBIS, 14, 83, 85
© Conor Caffrey/SPL/Photo Researchers, 40
© Corel Corporation, 28
Jeff DiMatteo, 26, 50, 90
© Reinhard Eisele/CORBIS, 70
Fine Art Society, London, UK/Bridgeman Art Library, 31
© Michael Heron/CORBIS, 65
© Hulton/Archive by Getty Images, 19, 32, 37
© Ed Kashi/CORBIS, 62
© Erich Lessing/Art Resource, 16
Library of Congress, 35
© Wally McNamee/CORBIS, 88
© Cordelia Molloy/SPL/Photo Researchers, 69
© North Wind Pictures, 24, 78, 81
PhotoDisc, 9, 13, 42, 45, 47, 55, 58
© Jeffrey L. Rotman/CORBIS, 56
© Stock Montage, Inc., 17, 22
© Jim Varney/SPL/Photo Researchers, 52

About the Authors

Pam Walker received her degree in biology at Georgia College and advanced degrees in education at Georgia Southern University. Elaine Wood studied biology at West Georgia College and received her graduate degrees in education from University of West Georgia College. They have more than thirty years of teaching experience in science in grades seven through twelve.

Ms. Walker and Ms. Wood are coauthors of more than a dozen science teacher resource activity books, two science textbooks, and a series of middle school books on human body systems.